CW00556161

One Life My Life

One Life My Life

Gina Interlandi

My Autobiography

One Life My Life
My Autobiography
Copyright © 2016 Gina Interlandi
Cover photo © photographer Diana Kirk
www.dianakirkphotography.com

First Edition

Library of Congress Control Number:		2016900919
ISBN:	Hardcover	978-1-0878-1765-1
	Paperback	978-1-0878-1763-7
	eBook	978-1-0878-1764-4

All rights reserved. No part of this publication may be reproduced, distributed, or transmitted in any form or by any means, including photocopying, recording, or other electronic or mechanical methods, without the prior written permission of the publisher or author, except in the case of brief quotations embodied in critical reviews and certain other noncommercial uses permitted by copyright law.

Printed in the United States of America

Rev. date: 06-Dec-2019

To order additional copies of this book,
contact: barnesandnoble.com and amazon.com

Missing you both every day of my life.

Dedication

I dedicated this book to my mother Josephine and sister Teresa. I thank my mother and sister for raising me the best they could up until the time they had left on this earth. They were two incredible women who were amazing as well as being selfless. I know they are both with God in Heaven, and one day I will get to see them again. Even though I wish they were both here with me and my family today, I do believe they are both looking down upon all of us from Heaven.

Contents

Dedication   vii
Introduction   xi

Chapter One   My childhood years   1
Chapter Two   My teenage years   9
Chapter Three   Losing my mother so young   17
Chapter Four   The five stages we go through   27
Chapter Five   My teenage pregnancy   35
Chapter Six   The birth of my daughter   43
Chapter Seven   Finding out Teresa had AIDS   55
Chapter Eight   Teresa battling AIDS   65
Chapter Nine   When Luis and I first met   75
Chapter Ten   The start of our relationship   83
Chapter Eleven   The loss of my unborn child   91
Chapter Twelve   When we got married   99
Chapter Thirteen   Why our marriage started falling apart   107
Chapter Fourteen   Going through my separation   115
Chapter Fifteen   Finding myself again   123
Chapter Sixteen   The beginning of my new life   131

Acknowledgments   139

Introduction

IN MY BOOK I talk about the struggles and the choices that I had to make throughout my life. The tragedy of losing my mother at a young age, my attempted suicide, my teenage pregnancy, my sister losing her battle to AIDS and the many other heartaches that have come along the way.

There are things in this book that I have never even told my family and closest friends. I was always afraid to tell people too much for the fear of being judged. I am now no longer afraid. In my belief there is only one person who can judge me and that is God.

My goal in life is to reach out and help other people that have gone through similar situations that I have gone through in my life. Hopefully I can help the ones that may be afraid to talk about their own lives. When you truly believe in yourself you can accomplish anything you want in life.

Throughout my life I made my own decisions, I made mistakes, and I struggled, but I never gave up, and in the end these experiences made me a stronger woman.

Chapter One

My childhood years

AS THE YOUNGEST of Eight, I always admired all of my brothers and sisters. I grew up in such a great Italian family (Salvatore, Thomas, Teresa, Michael, Nicholas, Johnny, Maria, and then me.)

The only devastating thing that happened in my family was eight months into my mother's pregnancy with my brother Johnny, she became ill with the measles which resulted in Johnny becoming hearing impaired. My parents taught all of us to love and respect one another, and for the most part we did. There were times we fought with one another, but it wouldn't be too long before we made up and worked it all out. We were not a perfect family, we all made our own mistakes. That's how we learned and how we grew to become a stronger and more loving family. Who would have known then that my life would have been turned upside down as the years went by? I had a lot of great times in my childhood that was filled with so many wonderful memories. There were times that those great memories would get me through my toughest and darkest moments.

Growing up my father worked a lot of jobs to support us and my mother stayed home and took care of us. We didn't have a lot of money, but we managed. We never had materialistic things, but at least we had each other and many great times. When my parents moved from Brooklyn, they had bought a house on Long

Island. The house did not have a lot of bedrooms, so my father built a small bedroom downstairs for him and my mother. There were only three bedrooms upstairs so we all had to share rooms. Holidays were my favorite because we were one big happy family, and no matter what, we were all together.

As the years went by, three of my older brothers moved out, and soon after that, my older sister Teresa followed. I remember the house feeling so quiet and empty. Being the youngest and the last child, I always thought we would never be separated as a family. I learned then that wasn't how it was going to be, even though they all came home to visit when they could. When they couldn't come for a holiday, I would feel depressed and lonely.

My sister Maria and I would finally have our own rooms. When she and I were younger, we were closer and got along very well and we only had each other to play with. As we got older we started to grow apart from one another, and I started to see that she and I were different in so many ways. She did well in school and was very athletic. I was a little athletic and I struggled with school, so I always needed that extra help. I knew it wasn't something to be embarrassed by and that it helped me, but I sometimes wished I didn't have to work so hard. Maria and I were always together. We made the same friends in our neighborhood, but she didn't always want her little sister tagging along, so she would tell me to go back home. It hurt me a lot when she would do that to me. So I would spend a lot of time with my mother helping her around the house. "Our" friends soon became her friends. I started to feel unwanted by my own sister. I knew she loved me and I loved her, but I guess she just needed her own space.

I then made friends from different neighborhoods. I found friends who liked to drink and liked to do drugs. I wanted to be accepted for who I was. I was just an average girl who wanted people to like me for me, and I began wanting to fit in with certain crowds of people. I am not proud to say that I tried drugs, but I did it because I wanted to fit in with these people that were my friends. I realized the hard way that being accepted that way wasn't worth it.

One time I went to a party that my parents did not know about. There was drinking going on and people were smoking marijuana. Someone asked me if I wanted a drag and I said yes. After I did it I started to act different and I couldn't walk right. My friend Jejie noticed that I was acting strange, so she came over to me to see if I was ok. I told her what I did, so she found out it was dust not marijuana that was in the joint. Jejie was mad and angry at that guy for doing that, but I was lucky to have her there to help me get through it. I wouldn't say they were bad people, they just liked to party all the time. Some of them were just like me – trying to figure themselves out. I am not saying that drugs helped me but sometimes I felt like I couldn't talk to anyone about my life – not even my family. I think if they knew I was doing drugs they would have been very upset with me, so I kept it to myself. That is why I did these certain things in my life. At my school we had different races and cultures, and I had a lot of friends who were different nationalities. I never judged other people by the color of their skin or the language they spoke. As far as I was concerned, we were all equal in my eyes. I could never look at other people that way. When it came to boys in school, the boys of my own nationality never gave me any attention or liked to talk to me. I felt that my direction went towards the Spanish and black boys who would give me the attention and they did like me. Later on in my life, my feelings for one certain boy would change my life forever!

Me and My Family in our home in Long Island NY 1970

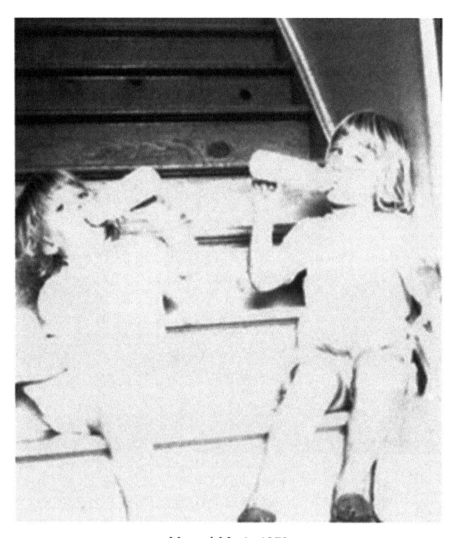

Me and Maria 1970

Maria and Me 1974

Chapter Two

My teenage years

IT WAS 1981. I Just turned thirteen and my life was going to change in the most amazing way – or I at least thought so. My brother Thomas came home to visit and he also brought his friend Nathan with him. This was the first time I met him. As I came down the staircase, Nathan was staring at me. He said, "Gina you're tall thin and beautiful. I would love for you to come and model for my agency." It was called Looks International and it was in Manhattan. I looked at him as if he was crazy. I never saw myself that way. When I would look at myself in the mirror, I would see the nose I hated and even my facial features I thought were less than beautiful. He had shown me a portfolio that had pictures of other girls that were my age. They looked gorgeous and so much older than what they were. After looking at that, I felt so much excitement inside. I thought how amazing would it be to look as beautiful as those girls. It was easy to convince my parents to let me start modeling because Thomas and Teresa both lived in the city and I would have both of them there with me.

My sister Teresa also was helping Nathan out with the agency. My mother said yes, but as long as my mother came with me. I was so excited and so happy because I finally had something in my life that I could be proud of, and that I could possibly be a full-time model. This was something I really wanted to start doing. I always wanted to go into New York City, but I was too young to travel by myself. I knew it had to be better than Long Island where I lived. Nathan started his modeling agency in his own apartment. It was so beautiful and big, and his balcony overlooked the city. Nathan also was a personal chauffeur for Diana Ross the singer, which made it very challenging for him to get his agency going.

I was very comfortable on my first shoot. I also felt I had enough confidence for the first time in my life. The photographer told me I was a natural and I was very photogenic in front of the camera. I spent a lot of time in the studio getting my pictures ready for my portfolio. The thing I loved the most was when I would model in the streets of Manhattan, there were crowds of people that would stop and watch me, but I didn't notice them because I was in my own world. I had two interviews with very well-known magazine companies. One with *Cosmopolitan* and one with *Seventeen.* The interview with *Cosmopolitan* went great, but they wanted someone a little older and I was too young at the time for the look they wanted. *Seventeen* did give me a job with one of their ads for an upcoming magazine. I was so excited – it was a dream come true for me. Then the weekend before I was going to do the shoot, Nathan called and said that they decided not to go with that ad in their magazine, but they would let me know when they could use me for a different job. Although I was very disappointed about the news, I knew in this type of business that would sometimes happen. I decided to take a break from modeling because my education was very important to me, so I took night classes to graduate earlier. Nathan was very understanding as well. He knew that I needed to finish with high school before I could pursue my modeling career full-time. He was not sure how successful his modeling agency would turn out but, he would want me to come back.

I started going into the city on the weekends to visit my sister Teresa. I was never afraid to take the train by myself, and when I would get into Penn Station, she would be there waiting for me. Teresa lived with two other girls, Marylynn and Lisa. They were all such good friends and they got along with each other very well. I always had so much fun and the best times with all of them. Marylynn was a ballet dancer and Lisa was a photographer. I always hoped when I got older I could share an apartment with my friends and be just like them. Teresa eventually got her own apartment in the same building on the 20th floor. Her apartment was nice, but the kitchen was really small. We always took walks around Central Park. One day we were behind Robert De Niro. He stopped at a newsstand, and we both didn't think he saw us but then he turned his head and winked at both of us! I was amazed and couldn't move quick enough to ask him for his autograph, knowing we were only two feet away from the biggest movie star.

In the 80s times were different, people were able to smoke everywhere and the clubs were easy to get into. As long as you had the right look and they liked you, your age really didn't matter. I was fourteen going to nightclubs with Teresa, and she took me to the Palladium, Rocky's, Studio 54. Those clubs would handpick you to get in, but Teresa and I would never have a problem being chosen. I always looked older than I was because of my height and the way I dressed up. I know I was in clubs at such a young age, but my sister always looked out for me and never allowed me to drink or do anything I wasn't supposed to be doing. I knew she would never let anything happen to me. Even though my parents didn't know about me going to the clubs with her, I would eventually tell them when I was a lot older. I never thought it was wrong. I loved being in the city and doing all those things that I had the chance to do. I would never change any of the things we did together. It was always our special time that I hold in my heart forever.

When it was time for me to go back home, I never wanted to leave my sister Teresa. I always wanted to stay with her in the city, but I knew I couldn't and as I would sit on the train thinking about when I was going to go back and see her it always put a smile on my face as well as excitement in my heart. I also missed seeing my mother and I know my mother missed me too. As soon as I would get off the train I would see her standing there with a smile on her face and I would run to her and hug her right away. I knew I was only gone for two days but to my mother it probably felt like an eternity. I was her little girl no matter how old I was she would always tell me that. My mother is the most amazing woman and she would always be there for me no matter what! She stood by my side and encouraged me in anything I wanted to do in my life and I would do anything for my mother. I never wanted to disappoint her, so I tried my best to make her proud of me, her little girl. In this world we think we're all going to last forever. What was I thinking? The most devastating thing was about to happen in my life!

Taking photos for my portfolio in New York City 1982

Me 1976

Chapter Three

Losing my mother so young

I T WAS JUNE 16th 1984. I could remember that day like it was yesterday. There were three of us that lived at home, and Teresa and Nicholas had come that weekend for a visit. Teresa and I came home from the movies that night and my mother was lying on the couch with her head on my father's lap and her hand was holding her chest. I asked her if she was ok and she said "Yes I am going to go to the doctor with Maria on Monday." She then told me to finish washing the dinner dishes in the sink. After I finished the dishes, I said goodnight and I love you to both my parents, then I went upstairs to my room. Saying I love you was something I always did before bed. That is how we were taught, because you never know what can happen the next day.

When I went upstairs, my sisters were already asleep and I went to bed. I had a clock in my room that I always looked at to check the time. I was laying in my bed when I opened my eyes and I was looking at the clock. It was 11:30 pm. All of a sudden I was pulled up by a strong force into a sitting position in my bed. I didn't know why, but I felt like I couldn't move. At first I couldn't even hear my father calling us, but then I heard the sound of his low voice calling for us through my bedroom vent. I ran to my sisters and told them something is happening to mommy! As they jumped out of bed and ran to see what was happening, I stood frozen at the top of the staircase. My mind was telling me to go help, but I was unable to move at that moment as I was listening to all the chaos that was going on downstairs. When I finally made it downstairs, I saw my mother laying in her bed with her left hand holding her throat struggling to breathe and her right arm next to her side unable to move. Teresa had already called 911 and Maria was doing what she could to help my dad. I wanted to help too so I got on the bed next to my mother and began to stroke her arm. I said to her, "It's going to be ok Mommy! God isn't going to let you suffer." Hearing those words made my father upset and he took me off the bed. I stood there thinking, how could I help my mother? Who should be blamed for all this? Was it my father who should have taken my mother to the hospital himself? Or the ambulance that took so long to respond to my house when they were only minutes away? I wanted to blame someone for what was happening, I just didn't know who.

My brothers weren't home at the time, and thinking Nicholas was at his friend's house around the corner, I ran there and banged on the door until someone answered. Through my hysteric cries I told them "I have to find my brother, my mother is dying!" They tried to calm me down, but I had to get back home. As I approached my house I saw that the ambulance had finally arrived.

I ran across my lawn as they pulled my mother on the stretcher. As I got closer I saw the sheet covering her, and her arm was hanging off the side of the stretcher and I told them, "Be careful that's my mother." It was at that moment that I felt my mother had passed away. My brother Salvatore was on his way, and my sisters and I sat waiting for my father's phone call to hear how my mother was doing. Then the phone rang. Teresa picked up and the tears rolled down her face. She didn't have to say anything, we knew what the news was. I ran outside – Salvatore had just pulled up and I held him really tight. I told him, "Mommy is gone!" I couldn't and didn't want to believe it. By the time Nicholas and Johnny came home, the priest was already in our living room. Although Nicholas knew what had happened, explaining it to Johnny was very difficult because of his hearing impairment. Once he understood, he cried and asked to see our mother. It was hard to get in touch with my brother Thomas because he was living in the city and not everybody had cell phones like they do now. He received the news from Salvatore's father-in-law John and he immediately returned home. My brother Michael was living in Louisiana at the time and we left a message at his job telling his manager what had happened. Instead of telling Michael to call home so we could deliver the horrible news ourselves, his manager told him, then told him to call home. Michael was very angry with him for being so heartless.

On this Father's Day in 1984, Josephine Dorothy Interlandi had passed away of a massive heart attack. She was only 51 years old. Our lives would never be the same, because this was our mother who meant the world to us. So here we all were, a family of ten, now a family of nine missing the one person we all loved so much. I can't explain the pain in all of our hearts. My mother was an incredible human being – a selfless, loving, caring person who helped people no matter who they were or where they came from. She was a Christian woman who gave herself to God. I knew that her spirit went to Heaven and there was no doubt in my mind she was in a better place. I never blamed God for taking her from me, I only wished he didn't take her so young and that I didn't have to lose her at such a young age. I will never forget the empty feeling I had inside, and I know the rest of my family felt the same.

The wake was the beginning of what would be a long journey ahead. My mother was such a huge part of me. She was my protector, caretaker, and my teacher. Following my mother's death, the days were long and the nights were even longer. I laid in my bed night after night with thoughts racing through my head. What would holiday dinners be like now? How could I have my sweet sixteen without my mother there with me? Who will take care of me? I was only fifteen but yet I was feeling so beyond my years!

I felt I failed my mother when I could not help her like I said I would and in my mind as I relive that morning every day of my life I blamed myself for what happen to her! I never told anyone in my family that I was blaming myself for my mother's death all those years and holding onto that was hard for me. I just did not know how to let go of that blame until it was time for me to!

My Mother 1948

My Mother and Teresa 1960

Josephine Dorothy Panucci Interlandi 1932 - 1984

Chapter Four

The five stages
we go through

THERE ARE FIVE stages we go through when we lose someone we love: Denial, Anger, Bargaining, Depression and Acceptance.

It was September 1984, three months after my mother had passed away. I was not doing so well and my father thought it would be best if I moved to North Carolina and lived with my brother Salvatore and his wife Joann. They only had one child at the time, my nephew Michael who was 1 years old.

I know at that time I put my brother Salvatore and sister-in-law Joann through a lot when I lived with them. But at the time I was out of my Denial stage and definitely in the Anger and Bargaining stage, and going through my Depression stage quickly.

Once I arrived in North Carolina, I enrolled in Carey High School. The atmosphere was very different there than what I was used to. Let's just say some people didn't like New Yorkers; especially my math teacher. He was so mean to me that he never even called me by my name – he used to call me a Yankee. Making friends was even harder for me because it was like two sides there – black and white would stay with their own race. No one interacted with each other. I felt like I was in the Twilight Zone. I could not even believe they were like that with one another. That made me upset!

I told myself I was going to make a difference in that high school. So I started making friends with everyone! I didn't care what any of them thought about "The Girl from New York!" I had no problem becoming friends with all of them. Let's just say everyone started becoming friends with each other after that and I felt like a made a difference and it was only going to get better.

Although certain personalities would clash, that is something you can't change. For the most part, a lot of people did find themselves getting along with each other better than before and finding out they had a lot more things in common with one another. In my high school in New York, I never looked at another person as being "different" for their color or their race. What was more important to me was how a person would act and how they treated others. My mother used to tell me, "Gina, the day God chooses to take us from this earth we take nothing with us. But if we can try and make peace with one another in this world that is something you can keep with you forever."

My nights were worse than my days. I would have nightmares about my mother's death. I would relive the night she died and how I couldn't do anything to save her life. It became so bad that I was afraid to close my eyes at night. I was prescribed sleeping pills to help me sleep and my sister-in-law Joann would lay next to me until I was able to sleep on my own.

One day I came home from school and Joann told me my sister Maria just called to let us know that our dog Pudgy was hit by a car and died. I was so upset. Why was this happening? First my mother and now my dog. I know Pudgy was an animal, but he was part of the family and I just couldn't deal with another loss.

I started thinking about my mother and fell into a deep depression mode. I just wanted to be with her. I missed hugging her, telling her I loved her, and talking with her. I didn't want to live anymore! I told Joann I didn't want to live, I wanted to be with my mother.

Joann was trying to talk to me and calm me down, but I didn't want to listen to her. I ran into the bathroom and locked myself in. As she was banging on the door for me to open it, I wasn't answering her. I opened the cabinet door under the sink and started to search for something to end my life. I found a razor blade and started to slit my wrists. Joann got the door opened and she started crying when she saw what I had done to myself. I sat on the bathroom floor and cried as she cleaned me up and bandaged both my wrists.

My body felt numb. I was feeling empty inside and I was depressed. I just was giving up. Why do I want to live? In my mind there was no reason for me to be on this earth without my mother. As I started coming out of my depression, I realized that my mother never would have wanted me to take my own life, and I knew God was not ready for me! I was a young teenager and I had a long life ahead of me. There was a reason why I should be alive, and I was going to find that out later in my life.

My brother Salvatore was upset with me and he had every right to be. I apologized to both of them. What else could I have said? What I did to myself was not right. In my family we were always forgiving one another. That is how our parents wanted us to be. They never wanted us to stay mad at each other. My brother Salvatore never told my father or my brothers or sisters about what had happened. Some things were better left unsaid at the time.

As the months passed, it wasn't getting any easier for me. It was my first Christmas without my mother and I sat remembering all of the good times we spent together, like when I snuggled under her arm on the couch watching her favorite show "I Love Lucy." My Christmas wish would be to have that moment back with my mother for just one day and it would have been the best Christmas present ever. In my mind I knew that wasn't possible. The only thing I could do for myself now was to keep my mother's memories close to my heart, and that one day I knew I would see my mother again.

I knew my mother was with me one day in church. When I used to go to church with my mother, she would always sit on the left side of me and put her right hand on my left knee and squeeze me, and it would always tickle me and make me laugh. It was one of her ways of showing me affection. One day I was in church with my brother Salvatore and his wife Joann. We sat in the first pew and there was no one sitting to the left of me. I was listening to the pastor as he spoke when all of a sudden, I felt someone sit next to me and then put their hand above my left knee and squeezed it. I stood still. I could not even move a muscle. I wasn't sure what was happening to me. With tears in my eyes, I knew it had to be my mother. Was God letting me know that my mother was ok and that she would always be there for me? I thought I shouldn't tell my family what had just happened because they would have thought I was crazy for sure! So I kept it to myself, feeling and knowing that it was my mother and that she was there in church with me even though it was only for that brief moment. I did not feel that I was alone anymore and that she was still with me in spirit.

I was searching for my final stage which was Acceptance. I knew North Carolina wasn't where I was going to find it. Back in New York, I was not sure if I could ever accept my mother's death, but I knew I had to try to move on with my life. It was the year 1985 and I had made up my mind. I no longer wanted to stay in North Carolina, so I finished 11th grade and decided to go back to New York

I was missing my father and brothers and sisters and also my school and friends too. I know that year I had made some serious mistakes in my life and I also learned from them. My brother Salvatore and my sister-in-law Joann had their own life and family after all. They loved and cared for me the best they could, but I needed to start my own life as well.

Me in front of my house 1968

Maria, Johny and Me 1969

Chapter Five

My teenage pregnancy

IN JUNE 1985 when I returned back to New York, I was so happy to see my father and sisters and brothers. I missed them a lot and I felt like I was away from them for years. I was happy that in September I was going to go back to my school, Sonderling High, and excited that I would see my friends and be able to graduate with them.

In October I was turning seventeen. I was not having a big party, especially knowing my mother was not going to be there with me, so I just had a few friends at my house with my family. At the time I was also seeing a boy that I knew I could not bring to my house because he was black, so I would see him without telling my father.

Another year has gone by and the holidays were coming up! I would get depressed because I was moving forward in my life. I still felt like going back in time and changing what had happened to my mother. I guess you can say I would always feel this way around the holidays.

This year we had Thanksgiving at my house, and after dinner I went to my friend Jeannie's house, who lived around the corner from me. Her mother cooked the best Spanish food and I loved it so much. As Jeannie and I were hanging out in her room, we were talking and laughing, and as I was looking in her mirror, she looked at me and said, "Gina you look pregnant." I then said to her, "No, I am not pregnant. I can't be, I was only with him once."Jeannie said, "That's all it takes."

As I was walking back home, I started to wonder if Jeannie was right. I was scared I couldn't go by my cycle because I would get it every three months. What she said stuck in my head and I had to find out if I was pregnant. One day after school I asked my friend John to take me to the Brentwood Clinic. I didn't tell him why I was going there, but he was a good friend and I trusted him, so he waited for me outside until I was done.

Back then they would test your urine in this big machine to find out if you were pregnant. The nurse told me that it would take ten minutes and she would check back in to let me know the results. When the machine was on I was watching it feeling so nervous and scared. If I was pregnant, what would I do? It was the longest ten minutes of my life. The machine stopped moving and the nurse came in. She then said to me, "It was positive and you are pregnant." I didn't know how to react to this, so I said to the nurse "thank you" and I left the clinic. My friend John asked if I was ok and I told him "yes" and thanked him for taking me.

When I got home, I went straight to my room and sat on my bed thinking about how scared I felt. I didn't know what to do. I could not tell my sister Maria or my brothers, and definitely not my father. I had to tell someone, so I went to Jeannie's house and told her that she was right and that I was pregnant! She asked me what I was going to do, but I could not answer her question.

I felt like I was living with a huge secret. I am seventeen years old! How was I going to tell my family and my father? I did tell the boy I was with and he was shocked as well. I didn't want to get an abortion. It would have been too dangerous at my age, and I was already in my second trimester.

The first person I told in my family was my sister Teresa. I would tell her everything that was going on in my life. I wasn't as close to my sister Maria at the time, so I didn't want her to know yet. I explained to Teresa that we couldn't tell our father yet or anyone else in our family, so she told our father that I was going to stay with her for two weeks since I was going to be out of school for winter recess, and our father was ok with that.

Teresa and I were trying to figure out how we were going to explain my pregnancy to our family. We first told all of our brothers and our sister Maria. Telling our father was going to be the hardest because not only did I have to tell him that I was pregnant, but I also had to tell him that the teenage boy who got me pregnant was black. I was scared of how my father was going to react towards this news. I thought he was going to be mad at me and that he would never talk to me ever again! I knew sooner or later I would have to tell my father. I was going to start showing soon and I had to go back home eventually! Teresa called our father and had to tell him over the phone. That was the only way she could have done it. At first my father was mad and upset with me and I could not blame him for feeling that way. If I were in my father's shoes I would have felt the same. I would not have been able to ever explain myself to my father. The words "I am pregnant" just could not come out of my mouth.

After talking to my father, I went back home to Long Island. I didn't want to go back to high school and I asked my father to sign me out of school. I figured after I had the baby I would go back or I would get my GED. Some of my friends knew that I was pregnant, but most of the other people that I went to school with didn't. I didn't want to be pregnant in high school, and it was also my graduating year. I was upset that I didn't get the chance to go to my prom or even get to do all the things after prom. Knowing

I wasn't going to graduate with all my friends was very upsetting to me as well. I knew I was going to raise my baby on my own with the help of my family and closest friends. I never planned on getting pregnant at seventeen! It was my first time being with a boy! I should have taken the right precautions but most teenagers don't think that getting pregnant would ever happen to them. A young girl needs to have her mother around so that they can talk about boys and how a teenager turns into a woman. I didn't have my mother to talk to about those things. I should have gone to my older sister Teresa, but to me it just wasn't the same.

My sister Teresa wanted me to come into the city for a weekend. She wanted to take me shopping because she knew I was in my sixth month of pregnancy, and I couldn't afford to buy myself clothes because I didn't have a job. After we went shopping, we met up with Cari, one of Teresa's closest and best friends. Teresa was her maid of honor in her wedding when she had married Sammy Ash. Sammy and Cari were the most caring and compassionate couple and they cared a lot for my sister Teresa, and for me as well. Knowing I was so young and pregnant, they were very concerned for my future just like everyone else in my family was. Teresa and I went to this little cafe to have lunch with Cari.

They were talking to me about this couple who couldn't have any children of their own and that they wanted to adopt a baby. They didn't care what nationality the baby was as long as the baby was healthy and came from a healthy background. The couple was willing to do it privately and they also wanted to offer a very large sum of money. Teresa and Cari asked me if I would consider giving the baby up for adoption.

At first I was shocked because I was not planning on giving my baby up! I understood why they were both telling me about this couple, knowing how I couldn't support or raise a baby at my age on my own without any money in the bank and not even having a stable place to live. It was a lot for me to think about. I felt bad for this couple whom I never met before, and I am sure they would be wonderful parents who were loving and caring and also wealthy with a stable home as well. I was not an immature young girl. I knew at the time I made the right decision and I chose to keep my baby and not do the adoption. I appreciated the concerns that my sister Teresa and Cari had for me. But adoption was not the option I would have even considered. Some people would think I was crazy, knowing if I would have given my baby up that I would have had enough money to go to college and take up something I would have wanted to do later on in life. I just felt that there was no amount of money that could have ever taken the place of me being a mother to my own child, and giving up my baby would have meant I was giving up on both of our lives. Yes, I was a young teenage girl and I knew it was not going to be easy by any means. I knew I was going to suffer and struggle moving forward into my future. I was scared, and at times I felt so empty and alone not knowing how my life would turn out to be.

Sometimes struggling in life doesn't always mean it is a bad thing! There are so many other people in this world who have struggled and succeeded in their lives and have their own careers today. The only thing I could strive for in my life at that time was to be a caring and loving mother, and try to be the best provider that I could be for my child. Only if I knew then that was going to be the hardest choice that I made in my life! In which I would only find out later on if that was the right choice I made!

Me in my backyard 1984

Chapter Six

The birth of my daughter

IT WAS JUNE 27, TH 1986 when I gave birth to a baby girl. I named her Tatiana Marie Interlandi. I have to say she was the most beautiful baby girl, and even the nurses went crazy over her. I had gone through twenty hours of labor and I had a natural birth. Seeing her for the first time – it was all worth it. I felt I had someone to love and take care of. For some reason it wasn't that scary to me anymore – it was more of reality that I was a mother.

My father had sold our house in Long Island and I did not have a stable place to live. I was on Public Assistance which helped me with rent, food, and medical. I was only receiving $500 a month from them and I was getting no child support for Tatiana so I had to do what any single mother would have to do and provide for the both of us. If it meant me having to be on Public Assistance for a couple of years then that's what I had to do. I never cared who knew I was on it, and no one should ever judge anyone for being on Public Assistance. Not everyone in society abuses the system, and there were other people like me at my age that needed it as well. I am not proud to say I was on Public Assistance and I wished I never had to be on it, but until I was able to get a good job and support myself and my daughter on my own, I had no other choice.

I was living in a very small studio apartment – it was like the size of a closet. When my daughter Tatiana was first born, I could not afford most things that other people could. I didn't have a crib for her so she slept in my bed with me. I could not even afford diapers so I did it the old fashioned way, I used cloth diapers with safety pins that held each side of the diaper. I'd rather have used the little money I was getting from Public Assistance for other important things that I needed to buy for Tatiana.

We only lived in that studio apartment for three weeks. I had to move because I couldn't afford the rent. So I had to move in with a friend until I could find a stable place to live.

A month after I moved out, I had seen in the newspaper that the house I rented that studio apartment in was raided. They had other people living downstairs who were selling drugs. I didn't live there long enough to know they were dealing drugs out of that house. I was glad I moved out of that apartment when I did, and I know God was watching over me and Tatiana.

Tatiana was three months old when I moved into my friend Jean's house. Her parents Bill and Rachel loved me and Tatiana and they wanted to help us. They were like my second family and I even had the opportunity to go back to high school and graduate in 1987. My friend Jean watched my daughter Tatiana when I went to school during the day. There was a certain amount of money that the government would allow for a babysitter. Jean would receive a check from them every week. That program helped me out a lot for that one year, and I knew I could trust Jean watching my daughter.

On Tatiana's 1st birthday June 27, th 1987 I graduated from Sonderling High School. It was the greatest feeling to finally receive my diploma and knowing I had my daughter there with me too. I was very upset that I could not have a big 1st birthday party for Tatiana. As long as she knew I loved her that meant more to me than having some party that she wouldn't even remember.

I could not afford to go to college after I graduated and I was trying to find a good job so I could come off Public Assistance. I moved out of my friend Jean's house and found an apartment with my brother John. It was in a basement, which was not what I would have liked to live in, but Tatiana was one years old at the time and it was hard for me to do it on my own. So I figured I would share an apartment with my brother and see if it would work out living with him. Sometimes it is hard to live with your family, and it was hard for me to live with him. So I went to live at my friend Susan's house until I could get myself into a better place.

I lived at Susan's house for a year after Tatiana turned two years old. I then found another place to live and I was able to find a job to come off of Public Assistance. It was a one bedroom apartment that had no kitchen just a hot plate and a very, very small refrigerator. My friend Evelyn was able to get me a job where she worked and since I didn't have a car at the time she would pick me up and also take me to drop Tatiana off at day care until I could make enough money to buy a car of my own. Sometimes it would be hard if she didn't go into work, then I had no transportation to get to work. The job was too far for me to even take a bus. I didn't like depending on other people for certain things, but most of my friends were like my family and they helped me whenever they could.

On Long Island you have to own a car. Even though there were buses, they would only run every hour and that was hard when you had a toddler to carry around. The job I had with Evelyn only lasted a year and I had to move again.

I was trying my hardest to keep myself together for my daughter. Tatiana was three years old and I was getting tired of moving all over the place and my struggles weren't over yet. I then decided to go to cosmetology school and try to see if I was good enough to start a career in doing hair and to make decent money. At that time it was three thousand dollars to go full time and the government paid half of the loan and I would have to pay off the other half when I completed school.

I had no other choice but to go back on Public Assistance while trying to find a better job and place to live. I had to rent a room because that was all I could afford. There were three other people that rented rooms there as well and there was only one bathroom. I hated sharing a bathroom with complete strangers and I was not planning on staying there long.

One night I went into the kitchen to get a glass of water. I turned on the light and I saw roaches and baby roaches everywhere, so many of them that I was so mortified that I went into the bathroom and threw up. I could not believe I had seen that many roaches. I never lived like that! I didn't realize that they had roaches because we had no use of the kitchen just renting a room. After seeing that, I called another friend of mine to ask if I could stay a couple of days with her until Public Assistance found me a place to live. She said it was okay, but she was also renting an apartment and she had to tell her landlords that I was only visiting. When I left that house, I took nothing with me I left my bed, TV, and a dresser. I would not even think to take any of those things after knowing how many roaches I seen. After staying with my friend for a few days, Public Assistance still could not find me a place live and they said I could go to a shelter. I would never go to a shelter with my daughter.

As a mother I had to make the hardest choice ever! It was the right choice for me to make at the time because I had no other place to go. I had to give Tatiana to my brother Nicholas who was Tatiana's godfather just until I could get back on my feet, and I knew she was safe with my brother. I was struggling more than ever and to put her through all of that was not something I wanted to do. After leaving her I cried every day. I felt as if I failed being her mother and it was torturous for me to leave her. I didn't know what else to do. I was homeless and I hated to even say that I was.

I stopped going to school full-time. I was going part-time so I could work off the books and I was more determined to do my best to get us back together as soon as I could. It was going to take me longer to complete the course, but I figured I could always go back full-time once I was living in a better and stable place.

Eight months went by and my friend Jean's parents Bill and Rachel wanted me to come back to live with them. They knew that I needed to be in a stable place in order for me to get Tatiana back. They were happy that I was coming back to live with them. They were always there for Tatiana and me. I appreciated their help knowing that I could now take better care of Tatiana and it was a more grounded place for the both of us to live. Tatiana was five and she was also starting kindergarten that year, so things started looking good for the both of us.

I then received a notification letter from Public Assistance saying I would have to either work for the money I was receiving from them or find a permanent full-time job on my own. I knew I would make a lot more money working for a company then what I was receiving from Public Assistance. So I found a full-time job and I was able to come off Public Assistance for good!

They also stopped giving us Medicaid and food stamps. They only wanted to give me twenty-five dollars a month for the food stamps. I thought they were joking! I told them I didn't need the food stamps anymore. The most important thing was health insurance for Tatiana. I didn't care if I had it for myself. So I was able to put her on a plan with "Family Health Plus" which went by what

I grossed a month. I only had to pay them eight dollars a month, which was a huge help for me.

For those first five years of my daughter's life, I thought about all the things I had been through and what I had put her through as well. From that day forward I said to myself I don't regret having her. What I do regret was having her at seventeen years old and knowing that I could have given her to that couple that really wanted to have a child and knowing they would have been able to give her everything that I couldn't and at that time as I was suffering a long in my life which was painful enough for me to put her through. To find out later on in my life I would be the one to suffer the most!

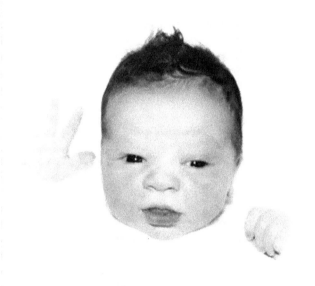

Tatiana Marie Interlandi 1986

Tatiana's 2nd Birthday 1988

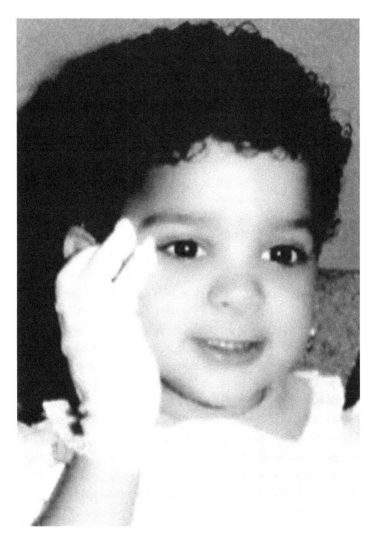

Tatiana on Easter 1989

Chapter Seven

Finding out Teresa had AIDS

IN JUNE 1993, I was planning Tatiana's seventh birthday party. I always had it outside in a park where I could invite everyone. That year was just like any other year to me – I would have some of my family there and my close friends and their children. I had a clown come to do face painting for the children and I also had other games as well. Tatiana was so happy just to have all of her friends there to share her birthday with her. As a child, Tatiana cared about and loved people who cared about and loved her, and that meant a lot more to her then receiving gifts. I wanted to raise my daughter the old-fashioned way, teaching her that materialistic things were not so important in life, but family and good friends were.

At times I thought to myself how could I have ever thought of giving Tatiana up and not being there for her? I love my daughter and I would always be there for her – no matter what life brings my way. Just watching her grow up was a blessing to me, and she was growing up too quickly. I believe God gets all of us through hard times in our lives, and I know He has gotten me through a lot of my own.

October 27th it was my birthday and I turned 25 that year. My brother Nicholas had a cake for me at his house. I wished I had all of my family together and my mother too! She was always my birthday wish on every birthday I had. At least I had my sisters Teresa and Maria, also my nieces and daughter with me. That day I was feeling a little depressed. I couldn't put my finger on it, but I was looking at my sister Teresa, and I just felt like something was wrong with her. She looked a little thinner than usual. I asked Teresa how she was feeling, and she told me she was fine. I then said to her you look a little thin. She then told me she was on a healthy diet and she lost some weight. I am very close to my sister Teresa, and half of me wanted to believe her and the other half didn't want to.

As I was driving home from my brother Nicholas house that night, for some reason I was not convinced that Teresa was telling me the truth. So I just let it go and figured if there was something wrong with her she would have told me.

Thanksgiving and Christmas went by so fast and then it was New Year's Eve. We were coming into the New Year 1994 and I was going to a party with this guy I was dating at the time. Teresa was watching Tatiana for me, so I brought Tatiana to Cari's house on the North Shore because my sister Teresa was spending New Year's with Cari and Sammy and their two boys. While I was at Cari's house, I was in her kitchen sitting at the table with Cari talking, and Teresa was standing in the other room with Cari's housekeeper. As I was looking at Teresa from a distance, again I just thought to myself, "Something isn't right with her." So I asked Cari, "Why does Teresa look so thin?" and she said to me, "Oh you know your sister, she has always been very thin." I then said to Cari, "Yes I know that, but not this thin." So Cari just changed the subject to something else and I didn't bother to mention it to Teresa again. After New Year's, I said to myself I was going to find out what was going on with her, and asking her was not going to get me anywhere. I would not get a straight answer from Teresa.

My sister Teresa lived in Astoria, Queens for five years, and she worked in New York City for a very well- known photography company that was family-owned, Fred Marcus. They loved her so much that they asked her to go to Eddie Murphy's wedding when he married Nicole Mitchell at the Plaza Hotel in 1993. Teresa also went with them to Donald Trump's wedding when he married Marla Maples in 1993.

Teresa was in a photo with the father and son in the New York Business Week article on how they started out their photography company. They knew Teresa was a well-grounded employee there and her work performance was outstanding.

On January 14th, I called my sister Teresa. She didn't answer, so I left her a message telling her I would like to come this weekend and hang out with her like the old times. Teresa called me back fifteen minutes later and she told me that this weekend wasn't good and she was going to be busy. So I told her, "Fine I will come next weekend." She said "Yes that would be better for me." As I was talking with her on the phone, I asked her how she was doing and she always told me she was doing fine.

On January 18th, I got a phone call from Teresa. She had told me she was in the hospital with pneumonia, but she was ok and she would be in the hospital for another week. I told her I wanted to see her, so I went the following day. When I got to the hospital, she was on the 8th floor. As I approached the door to her room, the nurse had given me a white mask to put over my nose and mouth I asked her why? She said so I wouldn't pass any germs to my sister. As I was entering the room, Teresa was sitting up in the bed and she looked fine to me, although she was sick and looked a little tired. I talked with her for a while, but I could not stay too long because visiting hours were almost over and I had to drive back to Long Island at night. Before I left the hospital, Teresa told me "Don't worry, I will be back home this weekend," knowing I was supposed to spend the weekend with her. I knew she would get better faster in the hospital then being home.

The following weekend came and Teresa was still in the hospital. The pneumonia had gotten worse so she had to stay longer. On Monday the 24th of January, I was talking to Cari on the phone about Teresa. She told me they were giving her morphine. I said to Cari, "Why would they give her morphine?" I asked Cari, "Please tell me what is really going on with my sister Teresa." She asked me to hold on for a moment as Marylynn was calling her on the other line. I waited for a couple of minutes, then I realized that they both knew what was going on with Teresa, so I hung up and got into my car and drove to my friend's house where I was living. When I reached the house, Rachel said Cari is on the phone for you. I said to Cari "if you don't tell me what is wrong with Teresa, I will call Marylynn and ask her, because I am feeling something is terribly wrong with my sister." Cari said to me "I am not going to keep anything from you. I was just talking to Marylynn because we both decided to tell you what is truly going on with your sister." Then she said "Gina, Teresa is dying of AIDS so she didn't want you or Maria to know because she thought she could get better from this disease." As I stood on the phone I was silent and numb and shocked. I told Cari, "I have to go." I went into the bathroom and turned the shower on so Rachel couldn't hear me crying. As I sat in the tub crying and feeling like I did the day my mother was dying in front of my eyes.

I asked God, "Please help Teresa. Don't let her die, she is too young" as my tears poured out of my eyes. I wanted to scream so loud, How can this happen to her and why? As Rachel knocked on the door, she said "Are you ok?" I came out of the bathroom and said "My sister Teresa is dying and I have to go to her." Rachel then ran into her room because her son died eight months ago from AIDS and my sister Teresa and I went to his wake in New York. At Andrew's wake, I remember I hugged my sister and said to her "Thank God no one in our family has this horrible disease." Now I could only imagine what my sister's face looked like when I said that to her.

I had to leave and tell my sister Maria what was going on with Teresa, but when I got to Maria's, she already knew about Teresa from my father. We both cried together. Maria said, "Isn't there something they can give her to make her get better?" I told her Teresa has full-blown AIDS and that her body was already being taken over by the bad cells. I didn't want to believe it either. I wanted Teresa to get better and come out of the hospital and everything to go back to the way it was.

My brother Thomas wanted Teresa to tell us because he knew Teresa was not doing well. I guess she could never get the words to come out and tell us she had AIDS, and it had to be very hard for her to tell us. The only people she told were my four older brothers, her three best friends, Cari, Lisa and Marylynn. The only ones that did not know were my father, Johnny, Maria, and myself. Cari told me that Teresa did not want me to know because she said if I knew, I would never let her live her life. Meaning I would have moved in with her and try to take care of her and I would never let anything happen to her. Teresa did not want that. She just wanted to keep living a normal life. She also told Cari that she was proud of me for growing into a beautiful woman and raising Tatiana on my own. Teresa was also happy that I never gave Tatiana up because it gave her the opportunity to help me raise Tatiana and knowing she would have never been able to have children of her own because of this disease.

Teresa, Maria, Johny, Me & My Mother 1972

Me and Teresa 1982

Chapter Eight

Teresa battling AIDS

WHEN MY FATHER found out about my sister Teresa, he flew up to New York the next day. That year we were having a lot of bad blizzards. It was hard to drive knowing all of the roads and highways were bad, but I did it anyway – I had to be with my sister. Teresa was no longer on the 8th floor, they moved her to the 12th floor which was the AIDS ward. Teresa had her own room, and knowing my brother Thomas and my father were able to stay with her at night made all of us feel better she was never by herself. There was always one of us with her at all times.

My brother Nicholas called all of us and said that Teresa wanted us to all come on Saturday, February 5th. We were all there except my brother Salvatore because he was on his way to New York. As we were all with Teresa that day, she was asking for certain things that she wanted like an Italian pastry that she wanted, and we got it for her. I was standing next to her and she was telling me what she wanted to wear in the casket when she passed away. I did not want to hear that, I just wanted her to get out of that bed! I wanted to take her out of there myself because I knew she didn't want to be there. I laid my head over her stomach as my tears could not stop. I wanted to hold her and never let her go! She wasn't only my older sister, she took the part of being my mother too. It was getting late and we all had to leave, so my father stayed with her in the room that night.

As the days went by, we all would go back and forth to the hospital. It was hard to see my sister like that! She could not even speak because she lost all feeling in her tongue. Although she had no lesions on her body, I still had to face watching my sister die of AIDS! I just had to see her eyes open one more time and I wanted for her to see me one last time, so I went to the hospital on February 10th. As I took her hand and said to her "Teresa if you can hear me please open your eyes." She turned her head, and her eyes opened for me one last time.

The next day the nurses said, "I can't believe she is still holding on." It was amazing to them, because Teresa should have passed away two days ago. I knew she was waiting for my brother Salvatore, when he arrived to the hospital he spent his time with her. I couldn't be there anymore, it hurt me too much, so I stayed in Long Island and waited for the phone call. When my brother Salvatore called me, I could not even explain how his voice sounded! As he cried, he told me our sister Teresa had passed away!

Teresa was only thirty-eight years old when she died February 12th 1994, and should not have died so young! If my sister didn't meet that guy, she would have never caught AIDS.

My sister had met a man in a club one night were she had lived in New York City. The man was a bartender at this club and he was attracted to my sister Teresa and why not? She was tall, beautiful, and had a great personality. In the '80s people met each other and sometimes without thinking would sleep with each other never thinking what could happen if the other person had a disease. It was not my sister's fault. She was a very intelligent woman. Teresa would never do anything that was not right – even to sleep with a man she did not know. I did not know who this man was and I don't know if he ever died! Some people could be a carrier of AIDS and never get full-blown AIDS like my sister Teresa.

While Teresa was in the hospital, I walked around the AIDS ward. It was very sad to watch babies, children, men and women of all ages dying from this disease. I met this man who I sat next to and I talked to him knowing half his face was deteriorated. It did not bother me, because he was a human being just like everyone else on that floor! What makes me angry is that some people who are not aware of this disease were ignorant and they thought if someone had AIDS and they were standing next to that person or touch that person, then they would catch it.

That is not true! Some of those people caught this horrible disease by blood transfusions, some people were carriers and gave it to another person by having sex, knowing they could give it to another person! When people would ask me about my sister they would not ask me how she caught AIDS! They would just assume and say "Was it drugs?" It made me furious how they would come to their own conclusions without asking how she caught this horrible disease! I would tell them she was with a man who gave this disease to her. There are people that have done drugs with needles that have caught AIDS and pregnant women who passed it along to their baby.

When other ignorant people were going around saying it was the gays that spread this disease, I knew this was not true! I have known a lot of gay people who died from this disease, and once again it made me angry, because how can other people point the finger at innocent same-sex couples? I have friends and cousins in my family who are gay and I am proud to say they are in my life.

I wish I could have changed what happened to my sister Teresa. If I could have protected her in any way I would have done it. Every day that goes by, I cried because I miss her voice and the way she laughed the way she smelled, the way she held me when I was upset, and now that closeness I had with my sister Teresa is gone. I can't go out with her and do all the things we used to do together!

What was worse, watching my mother die in front of me so fast and not being able to do anything for her or watching my sister Teresa die in front of me slowly and not being able to do anything for her? I felt like I failed and I blamed myself again knowing it was not my fault, but I was still blaming myself inside – I wanted my mother and my sister back. I just knew that was never going to happen!

At my sister Teresa's wake, I spoke of how wonderful she was and how I know she is with my mother in Heaven and that they are both looking down on all my brothers, me and my sister Maria. We had to meet my brother Salvatore back at my sister Teresa's apartment the following day, because he was the executor to Teresa's will. She had left some personal things for some of her closest friends, and she left some of her things to me and my sister Maria. She also left her nieces and nephew whatever money she had left over from her savings.

My brother Salvatore asked me to clean out her bathroom, because we needed to get all of her stuff out of the apartment. That was very hard for me to do. I felt like if I got rid of my sister's personal things that I was getting rid of her. I didn't want to, but my brother Salvatore said it had to be done. Going through her clothes was the hardest for Maria and me. We were the only two left to do all of this and it was not easy for us.

My brother Salvatore had taken some of the things that Teresa wanted him to have and he also took some magazines that Teresa had in the apartment. When he got back to North Carolina he was going through her magazines and came across one that was called "Young Modern Magazine." In the middle of this magazine it had a thank you card from a woman named Elizabeth Taylor who had written an article about my sister Teresa.

This was her last article she was writing in 1989, and it was called "Good Girls Get AIDS." Teresa told her story to this woman and all of our names were changed although she had one name for me in her article and it was Josephine which was my mother's name.

Teresa started out telling her story to Elizabeth about what her family background was and what we went through losing our mother and what symptoms she had before she found out that she was HIV positive, as well as how she caught this disease.

Teresa also spoke about Mikes, who was a Greek man she was dating at the time and how she fell in love with him. We were able to get copies of the original magazine from the magazine company, which made my brothers, Maria and I complete knowing we had Teresa's story and knowing how she felt and how she was dealing with AIDS.

Teresa had two large lumps behind each of her ear lobes. She thought she had swollen glands, so she went to the hospital to check what those lumps were. To find out that day it would be her worst nightmare, and I could only imagine the fear in her eyes and what was going through my sister's mind about how she was going to tell all of us. Teresa lived with having AIDS for ten years before she passed away. I had 25 years with her, and I wish I could have grown old with her.

Teresa 1956

Teresa at the Bungalow in NJ 1965

Teresa Interlandi 1956 - 1994

Chapter Nine

When Luis
and I first met

AFTER MY SISTER teresa passed away I felt so empty inside, as if I had no more feelings left. I was so close to Teresa and I felt so far away from my sister Maria, even though we lived a couple of blocks away from each other. Maria and I were still not as close as I wanted us to be and I could not tell her anything about what was going on in my life. I knew she would have never understood me the way my sister Teresa did.

Tatiana was seven years old and her Aunt Teresa was a big part of her life too. I had to explained to my daughter that God wanted Aunt Teresa now even though we also wanted her here with us! The death of my sister Teresa was one of the reasons why I did a lot of cocaine. Not telling anyone in my family what I was feeling like inside they never knew I was doing drugs. Back then you would never tell anyone you were doing drugs, you would just do them and hope no one found out.

When I first started doing cocaine, it was when I went back to work at the night clubs to make more money. I was a cocktail waitress and it was great pay and they paid me in cash! I always did it to keep myself up so I could make it through the night without falling asleep. I would not say I let cocaine control my life, I would not even say I was addicted to it. I also did it when I went out with my friends to nightclubs.

I had my reasons why I was doing it. It was another choice I made in my life, and it may have not been the right choice knowing I was a single mother raising a child on my own. I was afraid if my sister Maria and my brothers and father found out they would have been devastated.

There was one night I was in a car with one of my friends, he was someone who always had drugs on him and I was very depressed that night and he had a lot of cocaine on him. We both talked about how our lives were and what life brings us each day, month, and year. I talked about my mother and sister, saying to him why they both had to die so young.

I did so much cocaine that night I was not myself, I felt as if I was another person! I acted as if someone was watching me through the bushes and I was hallucinating. I was so high on cocaine I didn't even know how to stop doing it that night. I guess I thought I could handle it. I was wrong, and as my heart was racing so fast, I can't believe I got that far with doing so much of it without dying that night. I was so scared that he took me home and made sure I was ok before he left.

The next morning I woke up knowing it was a whole new day for me and I was not going to ever do that much cocaine again. I cried and really thanked God for watching over me. I went into a depressed state because I felt as if I found myself in another place when I did cocaine. As if I could live without feeling the pain with losing the two people who meant so much to me.

I was trying not to do as much cocaine, but when it was around me I did it. I never had to pay for it when I worked in the night-clubs. The only time I paid for cocaine was when I did it on my own with no one around or when I was with my friends. The friends I did it with were not bad nor were they addicted to cocaine. It was a popular drug a lot of people did in the 80's.

There were times I was scared and afraid that my daughter Tatiana would have caught me doing cocaine and I would have been very devastated if she did see me. She was only a child – she would not have understood what I was doing, but yet she would have wanted to know what I was doing. So I made sure I never let her see me doing anything while she was home with me.

I didn't think about who I could have hurt in my own family if they knew that I was doing drugs. So I stopped doing cocaine for a while and started looking at my life when I realized I didn't even have a social life. I stared hanging out with my other friends that did not do drugs. Knowing I could go out with my friends to nightclubs and enjoy myself and meet new people without having to do drugs was a good feeling.

It was Columbus Day weekend, 1994 and I went out to a club with one of my good friends. After a couple of hours she left and I stayed. Then I ran into my friend Evelyn's cousins Will and Ben while I was on the dance floor. Will told me Evelyn's brother Luis was with them. I told him I only knew her brother Johnny, but I never met Luis and asked if he could introduce me to him. When Will introduced us, we both went upstairs in the club so we could talk. I thought to myself he is cute and good looking and what attracted me to him even more was he had a strong jawline that made him look like more of a rugged man.

At 3:00 a.m. Will and Ben were leaving so Will asked if I could bring Luis home because they all came to the club in one car together. So I told him yes as long as he wanted me to. I guess Luis liked me too, or he would have never let me bring him home that morning. When I dropped him off he asked me if I would like to stay over but, I told him no thank you and that I had my brother watching my daughter Tatiana so I had to get home.

Even though he was my best friend's brother I was not going to stay with him after meeting him for the first night – I am not that kind of woman. He then reached over to me and gave me a really nice long kiss, which to me was a great one. So I gave him my phone number and he told me he would call me later on in the day.

Later on that day, Luis called me and asked me if he could come over around nine and I told him that would be great. When nine o'clock came, he called me again and said he could not make it because he didn't have a car at the time to come over I understood and just talked with him for a little while on the phone. He said he really did not want to have a serious relationship with someone right now and I was ok with him telling me that. I really didn't want to just hang out with him as a friend. I liked him so I just told him it was nice meeting him and I hope he finds what he is looking for.

The next day he called me again. I was shocked, because he told me yesterday he didn't want a serious relationship. I never thought he would call me again knowing I wanted a relationship, and I was confused with him in the beginning. Maybe that was a red flag for me, which I would have never known because I was never in a real relationship to even figure that out. I thought to myself, this is something wonderful and even more so because, it was my best friend's brother which was even more exciting for me, knowing he would be really good to me and treat me the right way. Evelyn told him I was a good woman and a very kindhearted person, so not to play with my feelings or try and hurt me in any way. When Luis told me what Evelyn had said, I was so pleased that she thought enough about me to tell her brother that.

Luis and I started going out and we were seeing each other almost every day. I did not mind my daughter Tatiana meeting him right away, because she was eight years old and I knew he came from a great family. Luis was great with children and he had a lot of little cousins and his brother Johnny's son Jovanny was three years old at time I was dating Luis. He loved his nephew so much and gave him so much love, so I knew he would be wonderful towards Tatiana.

Tatiana was a very well-behaved and a quiet child and she liked Luis a lot. He did not try too hard in the beginning with her because he wanted her to get to know him first. So he did certain things with her and for her which made me so happy that she would have a good man role model in her life who would be like a father to her. In the beginning he wanted to be a friend to her, eventually down the road he became a father to her.

Chapter Ten

The start of our relationship

FOR THE FIRST Year of our relationship, I knew I was in love with Luis. I knew he loved me too and our feelings towards each other were getting stronger. Even though we were only dating for a year, he wanted to be with me and he told me he would not be with anyone else. Anything Luis said to me in the beginning of our relationship I believed, and I trusted him because we both loved each other and I wanted our relationship to last.

When I moved in with Luis, he was living with his mother Norma and her boyfriend Willie. They were renting a house in Central Islip. We had the upstairs level which was nice because we had our own space and privacy. Norma and I had gotten very close with one another after I moved in and I felt like I was part of their family.

Luis worked a full-time job and I worked full-time during the day in an office, and I was still working on the weekends at the night club. Tatiana started elementary school which was right on the same block where we were living. After school, she would have to go straight home and wait an hour for me before I came home. One of our neighbors across the street was nice enough to watch out for her and made sure she got home safe. As a single parent, it was hard for me to work full-time knowing she was alone for that hour, but I had no other choice at the time. Tatiana was nine years old, and back then there were no after-school programs in that elementary school, and I did not have anyone who could have stayed with her until I got home. As a mother, you always have the fear that something could happen and you hope nothing bad would ever happen to your child. I wished I could have prevented what Tatiana went through.

One night while Tatiana was in the shower, something told me to go into the bathroom and check on her. As I opened the shower curtain, I saw bruises all over her back and arms. I was devastated! I asked her who did this to her, and she had told me about this girl who was in her class. She was bullying her and would make her do certain things. This girl was telling Tatiana to fight with other kids who were a grade above her and she would threaten Tatiana to do other things too. One day she made my daughter lay down on the train tracks and told her not to move. I was so upset and angry to think that some young girl could actually think in this sick way! I was so mad with myself and felt as if I failed as mother. I was supposed to protect my daughter from things like this! The next day I did not send Tatiana to school and I went up to the school in such a rage. I told the principal that I wanted this girl to pay for what she had done to my daughter. I went to the classroom to see the girl that did this to Tatiana, and the teacher let me speak to her alone outside the classroom. I looked at the girl and asked her, "How would you like it if someone bullied you? You could have seriously hurt my daughter with your actions."

The principal had her removed from the school. Even though there were only three weeks of school left, I had to do what was best for my daughter's safety, and I was not going to send Tatiana back to that horrible school ever again. I believe everything happens for a reason and that God was watching over us again, because the owner of the rental house where we were living had sold it and we had to move out.

We found another rental house in Bay Shore. It was brand new and nice, but it was smaller than the other house and there was not much privacy. Luis and I would argue at times and it was too much for me to do that in front of the family, so after six months I found my own apartment. Luis did not want to get an apartment with me because he was already renting the new house with his mother. Even though he always stayed with me wherever I lived, there were times when we did not get along, so he would have his own place to go back to. I wanted us to live together and there were times I would be upset about it, but we were dating for two years and I was willing to wait as long as it took. I never liked fighting or arguing with him, but he would say and do certain things that made me feel completely insecure about myself. He would tell me he was joking, but it really was not funny to me. He liked making me jealous all the time by saying things about other girls. When I would get mad at him for doing that, he would always laugh because he knew how upset I would get. That was one of the things I had to deal with most of the time, as well as the other things I was about to go through with him later on in my life.

All of my holidays were being spent with Luis and his family. We always had such good times, and knowing his sister Evelyn was my best friend and her family made me feel as if they were becoming my family as well. Luis came from a small family, which was so different for me because I came from such a big family. It really did not matter about the size of family, what mattered to me was that they all cared about and loved each other the same as I did with my family. I saw the closeness they all had with each other and love they had with one another, and that was what made me want to stay with Luis even more. Family meant a lot to me. After my mother and sister passed away, I always felt all my holidays had died with them, but when I was with Luis and his family, my holidays became alive again.

In June of 1996 when my sister Maria was getting married, Luis did not go with me to her wedding. I wished he did, but I did not want to pressure him about going because it was his choice not to go. In December of 1997, Maria gave birth to my niece Teresa Josephine. She was named after my sister and mother, and to be able to say my sister's name again and even to say my mother's name made me feel like they were still around. After my niece was born I became a little closer to Maria than I was before. As she was starting her own family and moving on in her life, I felt as if my life was not moving anywhere.

The only people Luis met in my family were Maria, Nicholas and Johnny. When we had my father's 65th birthday party, Luis finally met my father and my other brothers Salvatore, Thomas, and Michael, as well as my entire family. When we were around my family and friends, Luis would act different. He would treat me like a queen. When we were around his family and friends it was a whole other atmosphere and he did not treat me the same way. I never could understand why he would have a split personality. He could be extremely kind and loving, and then there were times when he was so cold and heartless. I did not share too much information with my sister or my closest friends for the fear of them judging me on my relationship with him. Luis did not start acting like that until a few years after we were together, and that is the only reason why I put up with him acting that way. I was in love with him, and what was I supposed to do? I would pray that he would realize what he was doing to our relationship and I hoped he would change some of his ways. No one could tell me they have or had the perfect relationship, everyone knows that, but when two people are in love and care enough for each other, they try everything they possibly can to make it work. I knew deep down inside that Luis loved me, and sometimes his way of showing it was when we were alone or when we were around certain people. When he would go out with his cousins, I was not allowed to go with them because Luis would tell me I always acted jealous in the club. Which was not true, and I felt the opposite. He would not treat me right when we went out together, and when you're in a club with your girlfriend or boyfriend, the other women and men in the club should know you're not single and you're together. Luis acted as if he was single when we were in the clubs, which made me feel like I was a nobody to him. I don't think he realized how much that hurt me. Even when he would tell me that I was crazy and jealous I would tell him, "But you made me feel that way all the time because of your choice of words and your actions." Most of the time, his family and friends would get a kick out of some things we would go back and forth about, and I would say, " we are a mix of Lucille Ball and Ricky Ricardo from *I Love Lucy* and Alice and Ralph Kramden from *The Honeymooners.*"

After eight years went by, it was June of 2002, and Tatiana was turning 16. Luis and I were in our eighth year of our relationship, and at that point of my life I felt as if I had waited long enough for us to get married and to start having a child. We were both in a good place in our relationship, so when I asked him if he felt the same way, he said he agreed. Luis and I went to a party in July of 2002, and after that party we both had an amazing night!

A couple of weeks later, Tatiana and I went to Pennsylvania with my cousin Renee for the weekend and it turned into the longest weekend ever. My car broke down in New Jersey on the way to Staten Island. The next day I tried to see if I could get someone to look at my car, but it was going to take a few days, so I stayed with my cousin Debbie. When I called Luis on Monday, he was upset with me because I never called him on Friday when I first got to Pennsylvania. I explained to him that there was no service out there and that was the reason why I didn't get a chance to call him. I felt bad. I should have at least tried to call him because he was concerned about me and Tatiana. On Tuesday morning as I was sitting in the kitchen with my cousin Debbie, I said to her, "I think I am pregnant." She looked at me and said, "Really?" I was feeling extra tired and my appetite was different too. The mechanic in Staten Island could not figure out what was wrong with my car, so my friend Lorrie was nice enough to help me get my car towed back to Long Island on Wednesday night. Luis was waiting for me at my mechanic's shop where I asked the towing guy to drop us off. I never said anything to Luis or Tatiana about thinking I might be pregnant. I bought a pregnancy test a while ago and wanted to take it first to make sure I definitely was.

The next morning after Luis had left for work, I was a little scared, but at the same time excited. After I peed on the stick I walked away and called my friend Lorrie. When I went back over to it, it said positive – I was pregnant. I was in such disbelief at first and then I was ecstatic. I ran into Tatiana's room and told her right away. In my life here I am sixteen years later and pregnant again!

Chapter Eleven

The loss of my unborn child

WHEN IT CAME time for me to tell Luis I was pregnant it was hard for me, because he might not have thought that I would get pregnant the first time we were trying. It was even harder for me to tell my family I was pregnant knowing we were not married, so I was not going to tell them until I knew Luis and I were getting married. The only one I did tell was my sister Maria, and I made sure she did not tell anyone else in my family until I was ready to tell them myself.

When Luis came home, I asked him to have a seat and I said that I needed to tell him something very important. I wanted to make sure he was sitting down for the news. As I sat in front of him on the floor, I took his hand as I started to cry and I said to him, "We are having a baby!" At first he looked a little surprised but he knew it was something we both wanted. Then he said "I love you and I want to be with you forever. Let's get married." I was marrying the man I loved, and to hear those words meant so much to me! Now I can finally say I will have my own family!

I started to tell both sides of our family that we were going to get married on November 02, 2002. I did not tell my family I was pregnant because I wanted to surprise them when they came for the wedding. Although Luis family all knew, because we were always over his Aunt Awilda's house and it was not a secret that we could have kept from them. His entire family was so happy for us, and his Aunt Awilda said we could have the wedding reception at her house. We were not having a big wedding; it was going to be small, but I still wanted to get married in a church. So when we went for our marriage certificate, they gave us a list of some pastors that I could call. We were planning all of this in three weeks – it was kind of fast, but it was exciting too!

Tatiana and I went to Lord & Taylor to look for a dress. I could not afford an expensive dress, so we looked on the sales rack and Tatiana came across a dress that was all lace and the color was ivory, which was fine. As she was walking over to me with the dress, it did not look like something I would have picked. When she noticed my face she said, "Just try it on, Mom." So I did, and it looked much prettier on me than on the hanger, and Tatiana was happy that I loved it. My stomach was showing a little so I had to get the dress altered. After I found my dress I felt as if everything was complete. I was more excited that our baby would be part of that beautiful day, something to tell our child when he or she was older.

I was only at my job for two months, and the only thing I mentioned to them was that I was getting married. I did not want them to know about my pregnancy, so I wore shirts that did not show so much of my stomach. There was one girl at my job, Damaris, who did notice and she asked me if I was pregnant. I told her yes, and I asked her not to say anything to anyone else at the job, and she promised me she wouldn't.

On Monday I was going to hear the baby's heartbeat for the first time. I was so excited and could not wait for the weekend to go by fast. That Friday afternoon after Damaris and I had lunch, I went into the bathroom stall and I noticed a tiny spot of blood on my underwear. Damaris and I were the only two people in the bathroom, so I said it out loud and Damaris said, "Gina that is not good, you need to call your doctor." After she said that to me I was even more scared. After speaking to my doctor, he asked me to come in right away so he could give me an ultrasound. I then had to tell the human resources manager what was going on with me. She told me that it was ok for me to leave, and that she would pray for everything to turn out fine.

When I got to my doctor's office, he took me into the room right away. As he started doing the ultrasound, he saw something that made him react. As I was watching the screen, I saw something that looked like a bump on the baby's neck. He took a big step backwards with his hand over his mouth, as if he had seen this happen one time before. I asked him what it was, but he could not tell me because he was a gynecologist, not a fertility doctor. When I got off the table, my doctor gave me a hug and told me that I had to go and see a fertility doctor right away. I was so confused, afraid and alone. Not knowing what was going on with me and the baby, I called Evelyn and told her I was trying to reach Luis, but he was working and was not answering his phone. I told her that I had to go to a fertility doctor and that I would call her as soon as I found out what was happening. She told me she was going to keep trying to reach Luis to let him know.

When I got to the fertility doctor, I was seen right away. As one nurse was taking my temperature, another nurse was asking me a million questions. I felt as if I was numb and kept thinking, "This is not happening to me right now, I just want some answers." I was waiting to go into the room when Luis called, and I told him that I was waiting to be seen by the doctor. He was working in the city and he felt bad that I was there alone, and I wish he could have been there with me too. The nurse handed me a gown to change into and said the doctor would be in shortly. The room was so dark and quiet, when the nurse was applying the skin tags onto my stomach the sound was up on the machine and I heard the sound of the baby's heart beating. She quickly shut the sound off and apologized to me right away. While I was laying on the table, my tears were rolling down my face. I wanted the doctor to come in and just tell me what was going on. The doctor finally came into the room and told me he was going to take some internal pictures of the baby. He took more than 25 pictures, and I felt like I was never going to get out of that room. After he was done, he left the room without saying anything to me. The nurse said to change, and that the doctor would see me in his office. I was so afraid of what he was going to tell me and that I might not want to hear it at all. I didn't have a good feeling about this doctor – he was not a kind or caring person, and I also felt that he had no compassion towards me. He told me from looking at the photos that there was a 75 percent chance the baby had cystic hygroma. I said to him, "What is cystic hygroma?" He said that it meant my baby had little chance to survive and that I would lose the baby within a couple of weeks. I could not grasp what this doctor was talking about; I just wanted to get out of there. How could this be happening right now? I called Luis and told him what the doctor told me and that I was going home.

When I got home, Luis told me that he spoke to his Aunt Flora who works for a pediatrician's office in Florida and that she researched what cystic hygroma was. She told him it was not good and that he should tell me right away what the chances were and what could happen. My doctor called me later on that evening and told me I had to go and get my blood drawn, so the next day I went to the blood bank and they took 19 vials of blood from me. It was a Saturday, so I knew they would not have any results until next week. My doctor also recommended that I should make an appointment with Dr. Kofinas, who was one of the best fertility doctors at the New York Methodist Hospital in Brooklyn. When I got to the hospital, it was a new fertility wing that Dr. Kofinas had just opened. I went into Brooklyn on that Monday with my friend Irene because Luis had to work but he also could not handle what was happening. I did understand that it was hard for the both of us. Dr. Kofinas was so amazing and nice to me. His personality made me feel so comfortable and I was at ease with him. More so than I felt with the other doctor on Long Island who was not so nice to me. Dr. Kofinas was so compassionate and he took his time while explaining to me what cystic hygroma was before he did the same procedure on me that the other doctor did. After the procedure he said he was positive it was a 95 percent chance that the baby would not have a chance to survive. He explained to me that 3 out of 3,500 women will be diagnosed with early stage of cystic hygroma, and it's almost as if we don't know how a zebra gets their stripes the same thing as not knowing why this happens.

Dr. Kofinas took a large needle and inserted it into my belly in order to extract a piece of my placenta so that he could overnight it to a DNA lab in California where it was going to be tested. That Tuesday morning, I got the phone call from Dr. Kofinas telling me the baby was missing a chromosome from the major part of the baby's brain. The baby would not survive too much longer, and it was only a matter of days or a week before I would lose the baby. He wanted me to come in for the procedure the next day which I choose to put the baby to sleep. I then asked him what the sex of my baby was and he told me it was a girl. I was three and half months pregnant, and she had a healthy heart but she was suffering with fluids running through her body and I did not want her to suffer inside me any longer. Luis took the news hard and could not handle seeing his first child put to sleep, so Evelyn came with me to hospital in Brooklyn. It took twenty minutes for the baby to stop moving after Dr. Kofinas injected her heart with a needle, and then Isabella was in Heaven with my mother and sister, resting in peace.

Leaving the hospital knowing my baby was inside of me and not moving anymore was the most devastating thing for me to go through. This was something I would not want any other woman to ever have to go through in life. Again, I felt helpless knowing that I could not save another person in my life. First my mother, then my sister, and now my baby. I had to watch all three of them all suffer and die right in front of me. Did I do the right thing? I started second-guessing myself, but it was already done.

The next morning Luis and I went to Good Samaritan Hospital. The same hospital I was born in and now I was there for my D&C. Luis laid next to me in the hospital bed until they brought me up to do the procedure. He had to go back to work and I wanted him to. Evelyn came back to the hospital to pick me up after I was done.

When I had got home from the hospital, I had to rest in bed. Then Luis came home from work to be with me and he told me that we would try in couple of months to get pregnant again. This was devastating to me and to him. I feel some people have to react differently to certain situations. Dr. Kofinas told us that there would be a 1 percent chance that this would ever happen to me again.

I never had a chance to enjoy my first pregnancy because I was so young. Now that I was older and more mature, this pregnancy would have been a better experience for me, and I was finally not going to do it alone.

Chapter Twelve

When we got married

LUIS AND I were married on November 2nd 2002 in a small church on Long Island, and we had both of our families and some of our closest friends there with us. On that day I thought I married the man I knew and loved for the last eight years. As I was planning on spending the rest of my life together with him and trying to get pregnant again, Luis was planning his own life without me in it.

After the wedding, Luis and I moved into a brand-new, two bedroom apartment in East Brentwood. It was perfect for the three of us, and Tatiana was graduating from Sonderling High School at the end of June. Luis and I were trying to buy a house in Bay Shore in the same area where my sister Maria lived, and I was happy about being closer to her and the kids. We had already put some money down on the house when I realized something was not right. I noticed that Luis was spending our money on things for himself and going out a lot. I would question him about it and he would tell me not to worry and that it was his money not mine. I said to him, "When two people get married it becomes our money, not just yours." We were two days away from closing on our house when Luis and I had a huge fight and he turned around and said he did not want to buy the house. I was so disappointed and depressed, thinking to myself, why would he do this to me? I just could not understand what was going on with him and why he was acting as if he could care less about me and my feelings. Even when we were trying to get pregnant, he would reassure me that it will happen again and that he loved me. I was not so sure if he was telling me the truth, but I just kept believing him because I thought he would never lie to me knowing we were married.

A year went by and we didn't even celebrate our first wedding anniversary. It's not like I was expecting anything big, nor did I ever complain about him buying me something nice. I was used to him not surprising me. Our anniversary was just another day for the both of us. I knew Luis had a good heart, he was just not that type of man to be spontaneous about doing things or going to the store and buying something. He would just give me the money and I would go to the store and buy what I wanted. It would have been nice for him to be the one to do it, but I never made a big deal about it. Maybe I should have. I used to be excited around the holidays and I felt as if nothing was going right in my life. Christmas came, and I did not feel like being happy and celebrating this year, and with Luis acting very odd towards me I felt like I was in this marriage alone. After the New Year, I felt as if someone needed to change their ways and it was not me, it was him.

Eight months passed and we were celebrating Tatiana's graduation and birthday party at Aunt Awilda's house. Since Tatiana graduated on the 25th of June 2004 and her birthday was the 27th we figured it would be nice to have it at the same time since we were all together. I was so proud of Tatiana and what she had accomplished in school. As I was standing there waiting to see her walk out onto the same field I walked out on for my graduation day, I thought back to when I first had her. I was this young girl who didn't know what life was going to bring my way, and now I was able to say that I made it far enough to see my daughter graduate from my own high school.

Tatiana was working two part-time jobs after she graduated and she kept asking me if she could get a car. She said she was planning on going to Suffolk Community College as a full-time student. I could not afford to get her a new car and that's what she wanted, so we went to the dealership and she was able to get a car in her name. The only thing I was able to do was help her with the car insurance.

Tatiana was so excited that she had a brand new car. It was a Nissan Sentra which was good on gas for her and she was able to afford making her payments every month, especially knowing she did not have to pay rent. I took care of buying all her food and her necessary needs. All I wanted was for her to start college like she said she would, and keep working at the two jobs she had. Luis was very upset with me for going with her to the dealership. He thought I was crazy for letting her get a brand-new car. I did not care what he thought about it – this was something that made her happy for once in her life. Even this time around I should have been the one to get her a new car. I always felt that I disappointed Tatiana when I could not give her something she wanted while she was growing up, and it was not a good feeling for me. I would always tell her, "There are five things as being a single parent I gave you: a roof over your head, food in your stomach, clothes on your back, I took care of you the best I could and I always gave you love."

Tatiana started out the first week on being good with her responsibilities and then she started going out with her friends during the week and weekends. I would tell her she had to be home during the week by 11:00 p.m. and on the weekends she would have to be home by 12:00 a.m. I always said to her nothing good happens on a Friday or Saturday night after 12:00 a.m. She was only 18 and was still living under my roof. She started listening more to her friends and what they were telling her. So she started lying to me all the time. When Luis said to me, "When are you going to realize you made a mistake letting her get that car?" at that point I knew he was right. I didn't realize she was going to spiral in a different direction as if she was changing right in front of my eyes. I was trying to control it on my own, and now I just could not handle it.

One Saturday night, Tatiana told me she was going to a friend's house. I asked her where did the girl live, and she said in East Brentwood, so I believed her. Tatiana knew what time she had to be home, but it was ten after 12 so I called her cell phone and when she did not pick up, I left her a message to get home. After that message I started to get angry and I started to worry.

She knew how I would get if she was not home by 12:00 a.m. Luis was out with his friends, so I was home by myself and I could not reach out to anyone in my family and tell them what was happening, I was too embarrassed. I waited for her to call me back, but the more time that went by, the angrier I became. I was about to call the police when she finally called me at 4:00 a.m. and told me she was out east in Riverhead. I went completely crazy. I just told her to get home now. I did not care about any of the lies she was telling me.When she finally got home, it was after 5:00 a.m. and I could not stop myself from yelling at her. Then Luis called me and told me he was going to sleep at his friend's house because he drank too much. I was so upset with the both of them. I just wanted to go to sleep and wake up thinking this was just a dream. Once I woke up, I wanted things to be back to normal. I thought to myself, "Am I the only one who is not dysfunctional?" I could not take it anymore – I just wanted to run as far as I could from all of this.

Later on that morning, Tatiana took off while I was sleeping. When I went into her bedroom, I noticed all of her things were still there, so I was relieved that she did not do something she would regret. Luis finally came home and I told him what happened with Tatiana. He didn't seem as if he was too concerned about it. He was acting strange towards me and I just could not get any straight answers out of him about what he was thinking or doing.

That Monday morning I went to work, and when I got home I walked into my worst nightmare: No one was home. I went into Tatiana's room and all of my daughter's things were gone. I was shocked and I could not breathe. As I fell to the ground crying, I broke down. I had to blame myself, it was my fault. Now my daughter was gone and I did not know where she was. My brother Nicholas lived in Nassau County in East Meadow, and he called me and told me Tatiana was staying there. Then she disappeared from my brother's house after a couple of days and she never went back.

Tatiana then started going into a different direction and she moved somewhere in Brooklyn. I didn't know if she was alive or dead and I did not hear from her for a couple of months. There was nothing I could have done. The police said she is 18 and of age to be on her own, so I had to just let her go and let her do what she wanted. It was hard and devastating for me to give her "tough love." I prayed every day that she was ok and healthy and I knew God was watching over her.

While I was going through my situation with Tatiana, Luis also decided to leave me too. He wanted to still be married, but he needed time for himself and he told me it was only going to be a temporary separation. I was hurt and upset, and I cried for days. When I realized I was by myself in a two-bedroom apartment, I had to figure out what I was going to do. Luis was still helping me with the rent even though he was not living there. I was not going to feel bad for myself.

I slowly had to get over my emotions and what they were both putting me through, as I continued to live my life every day not knowing what will happen next.

Chapter Thirteen

Why our marriage started falling apart

I FINALLY MOVED out of the two-bedroom apartment in August 2004, and I had to stay with my sister-in-law Evelyn. At that time she was buying a new house in Islip where Luis and I were planning on moving into an apartment in that house. Luis and I were still separated, and I never tried to ask him any questions about how long this was going to take. When Evelyn asked her brother what he was planning on doing, he said he was eventually going to move into the apartment with me but that he still needed some time. I kept asking myself why he would need time when I was the one who was being mistreated for the last several years. How could I be so blind to all of the hurtful things he continued to do to me?

The apartment needed a lot of work, so once I moved in I had to clean, paint and do all the floors. I stayed on Evelyn's side for at least two weeks before the apartment was ready. After the apartment was done, Luis then decided he was going to move back in with me and make our marriage work. After putting me through all of this pain I was feeling for last two months, not knowing where he was sleeping and living, I still wanted my marriage to work and I would do anything to try and make that happen. I just felt I loved him more than he ever loved me. When he came back I thought everything was going to be better, but it only got worse.

Luis was always hanging out at his favorite places, which were the local bars. He was there more than he was at home with me. Maybe if he put a little more effort into our marriage, and was not such a selfish human being who only worried about what he wanted, our marriage would work out.

Should I have blamed him or should I have blamed myself? I don't feel I deserved what was about to come my way, and thinking about it now, I should have done certain things differently in my marriage. Luis was good at lying to me, and as naive as I was, I believed all of his lies. It was a year later and we were still living together in the apartment. I was working a full-time job during the day, and then I started working at a part-time job a few nights a week and on weekends for extra money. Luis worked and was making very good money but I never saw a dime of it – only when we had to pay rent or bills. I could not even ask him where all the money was going or why I had to work two jobs. As he started being a little secretive about his life, I was going to find out what he was doing.

One day my friend told me that she had seen Luis at the mall out east with this young girl with blonde hair. They were walking into a shoe store, and my friend didn't see them doing anything as far as holding hands or giving any affection to each other. When I found out, I was working at my part-time job. Once I got home, I asked him about it and he told me that it was his friend's cousin. He made it so believable, and I was the foolish one who believed it.

He started making me believe I was the crazy one and that this was why our marriage was not going in the right direction. For years I was told by him that I was not good enough and I never did anything right in his eyes. In my eyes, I did everything he wanted me to do and more. I was a good woman and great wife. I always thought of him first. You could even say I kissed the ground he walked on. I guess I did not love myself enough to realize this was not a normal marriage or relationship. Some of my friends would look at my situation and thought I was crazy for putting up with all of this. Everyone knew that one day would come when I would eventually see Luis true colors and leave him.

I never was allowed to tell him what I felt, and when I did it became a fight. I could not communicate with him on any level, not even what we were going through in our marriage. My opinions did not matter at all to him, and there were times he would treat me like I was a child. He thought I should go and talk to a therapist because he felt that I was the one with all of the problems.

I wanted to go and talk to a therapist, but not because Luis wanted me to! When I went on my first visit to see the therapist, he asked me to talk about myself so he could get to know me and to find out what type of person I was. I was not ashamed to talk about my life or about telling him certain things that I went through growing up.

On my second visit to the therapist, he wanted me to talk about Luis and our marriage. After talking with him, he then asked if Luis would be willing to come with me on the next visit. I explained to the therapist that I will try and ask him, saying to myself, "Knowing Luis, he will get mad and angry about it and then tell me that he would never talk to a therapist and that he has no problems." I asked Luis when I got home and he looked at me and laughed and said, "I am not going."

Luis wanted me to talk to someone because he felt I needed to, when the therapist felt that Luis was the one who really needed to talk to someone. I never brought it up with him ever again. I then realized I did not need to keep on seeing the therapist. After speaking with the therapist, he made me see that I should start doing more for myself and how I should start loving myself a lot more than loving someone who did not care for me the way I wanted him to.

Two years went by and I was still feeling the same way about my life and my marriage. It was as if I was standing on the edge of a cliff waiting to jump off. Things were just getting more confusing for me every day with Luis. I was noticing so many little things about what he was doing. I found a note that had lipstick on it in his car, then I found eight graduation cards in his glove box. When I asked him about the note and the cards, he told me that the note was from his niece and the cards were for his friend's sister who was graduating.

One day Luis was sitting in his car and I went outside to talk to him. I had noticed this beautiful card laying on the passenger seat with some writing on it. When I went to reach over to pick it up, he took it and ripped it up, Then he told me, "It was for you, but you ruined the moment," and then he got mad at me and took off in his car. For him to act that way did not make any sense to me. If that card was for me, why did he have to rip it up? I started to believe he was losing his mind and he was trying to cover up any wrong-doing. After that day I just gave up trying to find out.

One day Luis was sitting in his car and I went outside to talk to him. I had noticed this beautiful card laying on the passenger seat with some writing on it. When I went to reach over to pick it up, he took it and ripped it up, Then he told me, "It was for you, but you ruined the moment," and then he got mad at me and took off in his car. For him to act that way did not make any sense to me. If that card was for me, why did he have to rip it up? I started to believe he was losing his mind and he was trying to cover up any wrong-doing. After that day I just gave up trying to find out.

I did what any wife would do for her husband: I cleaned, cooked, and made sure that I showed him every day how much I loved him and cared about his wants and needs before I cared about myself, and he should have done the same for me.

There is no wrong or right in anyone's relationship. It takes two people who could tolerate each other and trust each other enough to know that they could make it through anything in life together as long as they truly respect, care for and love one another.

Then that day came when I least expected it and I felt as if I failed again in my life. That moment when you know something is coming your way but you didn't think it would really happen, and then it does. Luis came home from work and told me he wanted a divorce – he did not want to be with me anymore. At that point he was right. There was nothing left of our marriage, and I felt as if I was going in a million circles never getting any answers from him and not knowing what things were going on behind my back.

I had no other choice but to stay living with him until I found my own apartment. Those eight months felt like an eternity to me. His routine was coming home from work, eating what I cooked and then he would take a shower and leave the house by 7 p.m. every night. I would not see Luis until the next day. It was hard for me to deal with that every day and it was not easy for me to sleep by myself knowing my husband was sleeping someplace else, and I could not say or do anything about it. It did not matter to him why he was leaving me alone every night by myself, when I realized I was already living by myself this entire time with him there.

Chapter Fourteen

Going through my separation

THE DAY I moved out of the apartment I felt as if I was leaving my whole entire life that I had with Luis behind me, as if I was never part of his life for all those years. Though my family and friends knew it was the right choice that I had made, I felt the pain in my heart that became numb to me. When you have to make the right choice in your life, you should never go with what your heart says – you should always go with what your mind is telling you. If I would have used my mind in the beginning of my relationship, I would not have put myself through any of this pain I was going through and what I was about to find out going forward in my life.

The next day Luis called me to see if I was doing ok, and I thought if he had cared so much about me he wouldn't have hurt me the way he did and he would have tried to work things out with our marriage. Luis and I were not legally separated, but he did what he wanted to do anyway. He thought he could come over to my apartment whenever he felt like it, then I told him, "If you don't want to be married to me, you need to pay for the divorce so we can move on in our lives." He felt I should pay for part of the divorce and I told him I would never pay towards the divorce because that was something he wanted not me.

A few months went by and things were not getting better for me living on Long Island. It was so hard for me because I knew I still loved Luis. He was trying to still control me like he did for all those years I was with him, so I called my brother Salvatore in North Carolina and asked him if I could move down there with them and he said yes. I figured I was making the right choice to move back to North Carolina and I just wanted to go as far away from Luis as possible. I was not running away from my problems, I just could not face the pain I endured everyday living so close to him.

I could always count on my family to be there for me and to support me in anything I tried to do in my life. I never talked to my family about my marriage, but they had an idea of what I was going through, and there were times when I was ashamed to tell them. They never got involved with my marriage nor did they ever judge Luis for all of the horrible things he had done to me. I wanted my family to see that I was happy and that I had a good marriage with him. For whatever reason I lived a lie and when it was bad and ugly, I made it look beautiful. At that time I just wanted my family to know that Luis was in love with me and everything was great in my life.

I told my landlord I was moving, she was very understanding and she wished me the best. I was planning on moving to North Carolina within two months and I would be there a week before my nephew Michael's wedding. My friend Jessica said I could come and stay with her for those two months instead of staying in the apartment and paying rent there. I was so relieved when she let me stay with her. I was still working at both of my jobs and with her help I could save more money before I moved.

My friends were always there for me when I needed them for support and someone to talk to. They never judged me, and if anything, they stood by my side in whatever I was going through in my life, especially when my mother and sister Teresa passed away, and now what I was going through in my marriage. I will never forget who my true friends are. They are not only my friends, they are like my family and they will always be family to me.

I was close to one of Luis's cousins Mary, and I asked her if we could have the family come together at her house before I moved away. Since they were all a big part of my life, it would be nice to see them all before I left. I wanted them all to know that no matter what happened between Luis and I that I would always hold a piece of their life with me in my heart and that I would never forget them. When I looked back at all the years I had with them – the parties, holidays and so much more – and with those memories you hold them with you forever. As bad as things got between Luis and me, it was hard for them to see a lot of what he did to me. No one expects for anyone to get involved in someone's relationship, even when it comes to your own blood. His family knew how much I was in love with him and how I tried everything to save my marriage! Was this all my fault? Did I let it happen when I could have just walked away? When you're in love with someone, it's not supposed to hurt. Being in love with that person should be incredibly amazing and that love should last until the day you die.

The last weekend before I was leaving, I invited Cecilia over to Jessica's house on Saturday. She told me she and Ben were going out to dinner and that they would try and come by, but they never did. The next day I spoke to Cecilia. She told me she had to tell me something and that she didn't want to lie to me. As she was getting upset and emotional, I asked her to tell me what was wrong and what happened? Then she told me that they were at Evelyn's 40th surprise birthday party yesterday. I was shocked that no one out of the family invited me knowing she was my best friend and my sister-in-law, even though Luis is her brother. I would have thought they could have put that to the side for one night and realized that we could have been in the same room with each other knowing we were all adults, not children!

I know that must have been hard for Cecilia to tell me, but for her to get that upset, something else must have happened, I just could not pick up what it was. Jessica came back from vacation and a couple of days had gone by. When I was getting ready to go over to Mary's house, Jessica said, "Oh you never told me about what happened with Cecilia," and I was also talking to my friend Lorrie on the phone. When I told Jessica and Lorrie they said to me, "Gina, there was a reason why you were not invited." I asked them "What could have been the reason?" Then Jessica said, "Luis had to be there with another woman." I said, "No, Cecilia would have told me over the phone." They both said "She is married to Ben and she probably would have gotten herself into a lot of trouble knowing that they are cousins."

I had to text Cecilia before I drove over to Luis's cousin's house, and I asked her if Luis was at Evelyn's party with another woman. She never text me back. When I got to Mary's, I did not mention anything to her right away, then I finally got the message back from Cecilia and it said, "I'd rather not tell you over the phone." Then Mary got a phone call from Ben and took the call outside, that's when I realized that Jessica and Lorrie were right. Once Mary came back inside I told her that I deserved to know the truth. Although she is his cousin, she was also family to me too, then Mary told me that he was!

I was in denial for all those years that he lied and cheated on me! The one thing I asked of him before we got married was to never commit adultery! So how could he do this, and why? Was I such a bad person? It didn't matter how much I loved or cared for him!

After finding out that Luis committed adultery, to also find out that it was not even a grown woman but a 17-year-old girl. I looked at him as if he was someone I didn't even know. I was disgusted and I could not even look at him the same way ever again! I was just in disbelief he would ever do that to me!

As I was driving to North Carolina, Luis was calling me over and over again trying to explain to me that it was all a lie and that none of this was true! I was angry, mad and crying to him and telling him why would you be with such a young girl? At that time I was trying to make sense of what was told to me, and I could not deal with talking to him. My heart was so torn inside over this news and I could never forget what he did.

I was not his wife, I was his puppet. I was the fool for letting him control my whole entire life. I didn't love myself enough and I was afraid to be alone because he would tell me no one would ever want to be with me! I didn't even know who I was anymore. I took the mental abuse for 13 years thinking he was always right. All those abusive words that he would tell me over and over again stuck in my head for all those years!

I once was that girl that was always fun, that loved to laugh and be happy about the smallest things in life. Luis never saw me for who I was and he never gave me any respect or compliments in what I did in my life. I just wanted him to care and love me the right way.

To see all my friends with their husbands doing all the things you are supposed to do as husband and wife. Luis never wanted to do anything with me or my friends. I stayed away from some of my friends because I never knew what to say to them, and when they would invite us somewhere, I would make up an excuse why we could not go. That was not the person I was – that was the person he made me become!

Chapter Fifteen

Finding myself again

ONCE I MOVED to north Carolina I felt better that I was around my family. I was so busy with my move there and my nephew's wedding that I had no time to think about Luis and what he did! I was trying hard to forget for the time being so I could get my life together. I knew I would have to eventually face him and get this divorce finalized, it was just not going to happen so quickly.

Michael was married on November 3, rd 2007. I wished my mother and sister Teresa could have been here to see it, they would have been so proud of him! Watching him marry Megan – the woman who he was going to spend the rest of his life with – made our entire family complete. It's happy occasions like this that brings any family together, and for just that one day we all forget those bad things that have happened around us and in our lives.

After the wedding all of my family went back home, and I felt so alone and empty inside when everyone was gone. While I was trying to figure out what I was going to do for work and where I would eventually live was a little scary for me knowing I did not want to be by myself. It was hard for me to get used to being in North Carolina. I found my first job in a retail store, which I was not making enough money to live on my own. I was there for just two months and then I found a job in an office that paid me more money.

Living in North Carolina was very difficult for me. I would try to keep myself busy every day, but there was nothing for me to do here. The women that I met at my job were nice but they were more to themselves and they seemed to not want to make friends. I spent most of my time with my sister-in-law Joann. Even though I loved spending time with her, I still needed to start my own life and I had no social life out here. I had more of a social life in New York with all of my friends, but now that part of my life had been completely wiped away from me!

Two months had passed and I was with all of my family at a New Year's Eve party. I was very happy to be with all of them knowing that it was the first time in so many years that I had gotten a chance to bring in the New Year 2008 with all of them. I also missed being there in New York that night with all my family and friends! Once the ball dropped and midnight hit, I knew I didn't want to live in North Carolina anymore.

I told my brother Salvatore that I decided to move back to New York. I knew he was going to be upset with me because I was not giving myself enough time to at least get used to living in North Carolina. I can't go back and change what has happened in my life but I can only try and improve it going forward! Luis was constantly calling me and trying to convince me that he was no longer with that young girl. I was not deaf to all of his lies and even though people were telling me he was still with this young girl, I know it was true! Sometimes people have to see things for themselves in order to really believe it, and when I was in New York I did.

Living in North Carolina for the past eight months gave me so much time to think about my life and how I was able to put all of the pieces to my puzzle with Luis together. I think back when I found blonde hair on his clothes, the note and all the cards that were in his car, all the nights he didn't come home because he said he was too drunk to drive. At that time I didn't want to face what I was seeing in front of my eyes so I just pretended it was not happening.

When I finally moved back to New York at the end of June 2008, I moved into an apartment that I found through a friend of mine. I felt more at ease and complete with my life when I moved back home, and it only took me a month to find a good job. Knowing I was around my family and friends again, I hoped that it can only get better for me now! As long as Luis could stay out of my life, I would be fine. He just would not give up and he kept on trying to get back together with me. He was trying to be strong and to have control but my feelings towards him were always stronger.

I can't understand why Luis would think I would want to be with him again knowing what he had put me through while he was having a relationship with this young girl for the past four years of our marriage! He said he changed and that he wanted to be with me again. He knew I was a great wife and he appreciated all of things I did for him for the past fourteen years of our lives. He said he was sorry for all the things he had done to me and that he would never hurt me again!

My emotions took over as I started believing Luis again, and when some of my friends heard I was going to give him another chance, they thought I was crazy for believing him! I still loved him and I was trying to forgive him for what he did. I believe if we don't forgive other people for what they have done to us, then how could God forgive us for what we do every day in our own lives? No one is perfect but God in this world we live in, and we all have our own faults in life. God knows I will figure out if Luis is telling me the truth or not!

I decided to give Luis another chance because we were still married. He was coming over every day, and it was a little different in the beginning as we were trying to work on our relationship again. I would not live with him until I knew for sure that he was being faithful and honest in everything he was saying and doing. I did not want to get hurt again, so I made sure I had my guard up at all times.

In January of 2010, when the economy crashed, the job I worked at was downsizing and I lost my job. I didn't know what I was going to do. I was paying such high rent where I was living and I was on unemployment. I was not going to survive, so I had to look for another place to live.

I eventually found an apartment through one of my friends, and although it was a basement apartment, it was new and it was a little less than what I was paying for the other apartment. I moved in at the end of June 2010. After I got settled there, Luis was coming over and still in my life.

Then two weeks after 4th of July, I got a phone call from a friend who noticed some pictures on Facebook, and I was told to go on there and look at them. I said to my friend, "Just tell me what you saw," but my friend said, "I rather you see it for yourself." I know most of the family knew I was seeing Luis again but even though I never really spoke about it with anyone of them. I did not want to get them involved, especially if things did not work out again for Luis and me. I had a bad feeling it was something I was not going to like, but if I don't see it for myself and forget about it then I would be the foolish one not to have listened to my friend. When I looked on Facebook, I saw Luis standing in two pictures with that young girl!

He never stopped seeing that young girl. I was so mad at myself for giving him another chance, why was I so stupid? Once a liar and a cheater they're always going to be a liar and a cheater! I had enough of being hurt by him, and even though I let him back into my life it did not mean I would keep that door open for him so he could come and go as he pleased. He denies everything that happens in his life to make himself look good, and I know Luis can never tell the truth.

I was trying to keep myself from feeling depressed again, and I told him I did not want to see him. I didn't even know what to say to him anymore. I felt so drained from all of this craziness that I just wanted to be left alone and to have some of my sanity and respect back for myself.

The girl that I was renting from told me she had a friend that was trying to find a good home for her daughter's teacup Yorkie, and his name was Milo. He only weighed 4 pounds and he was three years old. The first time I saw him I fell in love with him right away. I always wanted a dog like that but I could never afford one. She was willing to give him to me knowing I would take good care of him. They bought Milo from a mill out east, and the woman who sold them for $1,500.00 each knew they were all sick puppies. To find out that all of his brothers and sisters never made it and died! After they had bought Milo, three months later he had a seizure and they had to rush him to the animal hospital. The vet said to them his liver was not good and he would have to be on medication everyday which will keep him alive.

After hearing that story, it did not bother me that Milo was a sick dog, it amazed me that he was the only one that survived! I felt he needed someone in his life who could love and care for him every day, and I felt that I needed him in my life as well. It's true when they say animals give us human's unconditional love, and Milo did fill that loneliness of my broken heart!

When I first got Milo in 2010

Chapter Sixteen

The beginning
of my new life

O N JANUARY 1ST 2011, I moved into a small studio apartment by the water in Lindenhurst and I was renting from someone I knew. Kate didn't mind that I had Milo, when most places don't allow animals. As I was still looking for work, I was able to afford living there and I was just getting by with all of my other finances too.

This was the year that I had made a promise to myself that I would stop putting Luis before me and that I would start loving and caring more about what I wanted for my life! With all that I had been through with him, I was finally starting to lose the love I had for him and I was strong enough to file for the divorce. Even though I fought a long battle with my feelings towards him, I knew I no longer wanted to be married. Suddenly all of the pain I was feeling was gone, like a weight was lifted from me and I could start living my own life again, free from all of the abuse!

I cried enough tears over him and I became a stronger woman every day that went by. As I didn't care as much about him anymore, he came to realize that I was not the same woman who he first met. I did not have any hate towards him, although I would never forget what he has done to me and my life. I would not say he did not love me or care for me in a certain way, but Luis was never in love with me. I feel he will never fall in love with any other woman that comes into his life because of his own insecurities that he has. I just pray that he does not put anyone else through what he put me through, and that one day he realizes that and he does not find himself alone!

The only thing that I regret having to go through in this marriage was putting my daughter to sleep! I know now going forward into my future that I will never let another man scar me and my life the way Luis did!

On July 22, 2011 I was in a very bad car accident. While I was able to get myself out of the car, I was thinking how blessed I was – I could have been killed in this accident! I was so relieved I had my seat belt on. I was scared and in shock. I did not have any broken bones and no fractures, but I did have some pain in the back of my head, my knees were badly bruised and both my wrists had major cuts from the airbag that went off. God was watching over me and he protected me in that car accident; it was definitely not my time to go.

After the car accident, I thought that was the only thing left that could have happened to me, but then I was told we had to evacuate because Hurricane Irene was on her way. On August 20, 2011 the storm came. All of my things, and the apartment were destroyed. I then had to go and stay with friends for three months. The entire bottom half of the house had to be redone. Once it was finished it was beautiful, and I was back in my apartment and working again.

Each day that went by I was waiting on getting that final paper from the courts I felt as if that divorce paper would have been the last thing to help me move on and it would be one less thing to worry about. People who go through divorce every day must feel like I do, and I did not own a house with Luis, and we did not have any children. I could only imagine other couples that had a house and children, if it was hard for me it must have been even harder for them. It's not easy for certain people to have to stay in an unhealthy marriage for their children, especially when they are the ones who suffer the most! I believe there are so many others like myself that did not want a divorce, but how can you stay in a marriage if the other person will never try to change?

I finally received the envelope that I had been waiting for all these months. As I opened it and saw the date April 27th 2012, my eyes teared up. I remembered when I was pregnant ten years ago, that was the month and day the doctor had given me as my due date! Isabella would have been nine years old. When I think about it now, I will always wonder what she would have become in life. Sometimes it makes me feel sad, and I know I will always feel this way.

I think about why God took my mother from me when I was only 15, then my sister Teresa when I was 25 and then he took my unborn child from me at the age of 34. I would never question God's reason for taking them. I just try to figure out why? I do believe that God will keep on helping me through my life, as I know He listens to all of my prayers and even though I lived a hard life, He has been there for me every step of the way!

The choices I made through my life were my choices. I don't blame anyone but myself. My struggles of being a teenager as I was a child myself trying to raise my own child was extremely hard and at times painful! I was not proud of doing drugs and other certain things that I did in my past and God knows I have made a lot of mistakes that I could not go back and change in my life. The fears that I had were the fears that hurt me every day, and when I thought how can people judge me or my life if they don't really know me? How could people judge others when they don't know what that other person has gone through themselves? If people cared more for each other and there was not so much hate and judgment towards each other in this world we live in, I believe that we would all live a peaceful life!

God brings us this one life we have and it was my life. Although I can't say what the rest of my life will bring me or what path God will lead me to in my life, I know He will stay with me as long as I believe in Him. When I prayed to God for something, He did answer me with what I asked for. I guess you will all have to eventually find out what that is for yourself.

Me and my Family in 2014
Nicholas, Johnny, Thomas, Gina, Salvatore, Maria & Michael

Acknowledgments

I THANK GOD for the title of my book and for giving me the strength so I could write it. As god started to put all the right people in my life while I was writing my book. My friend Jessica Tomas who listened to me and inspired me, Maggie Wignal for introducing me to Author Alysia Stern.

After meeting Alysia, she said to me that I would have to relive my life all over again and become that book. She then introduced me to my editor Helena Noelle. After reading the first three chapters of my book, Helena felt as if she knew me my entire life. Helena started putting my story together, she said that my book would help so many others and be successful one day. I was fortunate to have met Helena and I was happy she was part of my journey and my book.

I am thankful and blessed for having an amazing family that has always supported me in whatever I do. My father, brothers and sister have been there for me whenever I needed them the most and for that I will always be grateful for them.

I am thankful for the great friends that I have in my life today and the friends that I have met throughout my life. I will always be appreciative for their kindness and support.

CPSIA information can be obtained
at www.ICGtesting.com
Printed in the USA
LVHW071916240220
648020LV00023B/1991